T0073471

Understanding Large Language Models

Learning Their Underlying Concepts and Technologies

Thimira Amaratunga

Apress®

Understanding Large Language Models: Learning Their Underlying Concepts and Technologies

Thimira Amaratunga
Nugegoda, Sri Lanka

ISBN-13 (pbk): 979-8-8688-0016-0   ISBN-13 (electronic): 979-8-8688-0017-7
https://doi.org/10.1007/979-8-8688-0017-7

Managing Director, Apress Media LLC: Welmoed Spahr
Acquisitions Editor: Smriti Srivastava
Development Editor: Laura Berendson
Editorial Project Manager: Shaul Elson

Cover designed by eStudioCalamar

Cover image designed by Cai Fang from Unsplash

Distributed to the book trade worldwide by Springer Science+Business Media New York, 1 New York Plaza, Suite 4600, New York, NY 10004-1562, USA. Phone 1-800-SPRINGER, fax (201) 348-4505, e-mail orders-ny@springer-sbm.com, or visit www.springeronline.com. Apress Media, LLC is a California LLC and the sole member (owner) is Springer Science + Business Media Finance Inc (SSBM Finance Inc). SSBM Finance Inc is a **Delaware** corporation.

For information on translations, please e-mail booktranslations@springernature.com; for reprint, paperback, or audio rights, please e-mail bookpermissions@springernature.com.

Apress titles may be purchased in bulk for academic, corporate, or promotional use. eBook versions and licenses are also available for most titles. For more information, reference our Print and eBook Bulk Sales web page at http://www.apress.com/bulk-sales.

Any source code or other supplementary material referenced by the author in this book is available to readers on GitHub. For more detailed information, please visit https://www.apress.com/gp/services/source-code.

Paper in this product is recyclable

Dedicated to all who push the boundaries of knowledge.

Table of Contents

About the Author

 **Thimira Amaratunga** is a senior software architect at Pearson PLC Sri Lanka with more than 15 years of industry experience. He is also an inventor, author, and researcher in the AI, machine learning, deep learning in education, and computer vision domains.

Thimira has a master's of science degree in computer science and a bachelor's degree in information technology from the University of Colombo, Sri Lanka. He is also a TOGAF-certified enterprise architect.

He has filed three patents in the fields of dynamic neural networks and semantics for online learning platforms. He has published three books on deep learning and computer vision.

Connect with him on LinkedIn: `https://www.linkedin.com/in/ thimira-amaratunga`.

About the Technical Reviewer

Kasam Shaikh is a prominent figure in India's artificial intelligence landscape, holding the distinction of being one of the country's first four Microsoft Most Valuable Professionals (MVPs) in AI. Currently serving as a senior architect at Capgemini, Kasam boasts an impressive track record as an author, having written five best-selling books dedicated to Azure and AI technologies. Beyond his writing endeavors, Kasam is recognized as a Microsoft Certified Trainer (MCT) and influential tech YouTuber (@mekasamshaikh). He also leads the largest online Azure AI community, known as DearAzure | Azure INDIA, and is a globally renowned AI speaker. His commitment to knowledge sharing extends to contributions to Microsoft Learn, where he plays a pivotal role.

Within the realm of AI, Kasam is a respected subject-matter expert (SME) in generative AI for the cloud, complementing his role as a senior cloud architect. He actively promotes the adoption of No Code and Azure OpenAI solutions and possesses a strong foundation in hybrid and cross-cloud practices. Kasam's versatility and expertise make him an invaluable asset in the rapidly evolving landscape of technology, contributing significantly to the advancement of Azure and AI.

In summary, Kasam is a multifaceted professional who excels in both technical expertise and knowledge dissemination. His contributions span writing, training, community leadership, public speaking, and architecture, establishing him as a true luminary in the world of Azure and AI.

Acknowledgments

The idea for this book came during my journey to understand the latest developments in AI. In creating this book, I want to help others who seek the same knowledge. Although this was my fourth book, it took a lot of work. Luckily, I received support from many individuals along the way, for whom I would like to express my sincere gratitude.

First, I would like to thank the team at Apress: Smriti Srivastava, Sowmya Thodur, Laura Berendson, Shaul Elson, Mark Powers, Joseph Quatela, Kasam Shaikh, Linthaa Muralidharan, and everyone involved in the editing and publishing of this book.

To my loving wife, Pramitha. Thank you for the encouragement and the motivation given from the inception of the idea to its completion. Completing this might not have been possible without your support through the long hours and days spent writing and perfecting this book.

To my colleagues and managers at Pearson PLC, who have guided me throughout the years, I am grateful for your guidance and encouragement.

Finally, to my parents and sister, thank you for your endless support throughout the years.

Preface

Today, finding someone who hasn't heard of ChatGPT, the AI chatbot that took the world by storm, is hard. ChatGPT—and its competitors such as Google Bard, Microsoft Bing Chat, etc.—are part of a broader area in AI known as *large language models* (LLMs). LLMs are the latest frontier in AI, resulting from recent research into natural language processing (NLP) and deep learning. However, the immense popularity these applications have gained has created some concerns and misconceptions around them because of a lack of understanding of what they truly are.

Understanding the concepts behind this new technology, including how it evolved, and addressing the misconceptions and genuine concerns around it are crucial for us to bring out its full potential. Therefore, this book was designed to provide a crucial overall understanding of large language models.

In this book, you will do the following:

- Learn the history of AI and NLP leading up to large language models

- Learn the core concepts of NLP that help define LLMs

- Look at the transformer architecture, a turning point in NLP research

- See what makes LLMs special

- Understand the architectures of popular LLM applications

- Read about the concerns, threats, misconceptions, and opportunities presented by using LLMs

This is not a coding book. However, this book will provide a strong foundation for understanding LLMs as you take your first steps toward them.

CHAPTER 1

Introduction

It was late 2022. Reports were coming in about a new AI that had human-like conversational skills and seemingly infinite knowledge. Not only was it able to articulate answers to a large number of subject domains such as science, technology, history, and philosophy, it was able to elaborate on the answers it gave and perform meaningful follow-up conversations about them.

This was ChatGPT, a large language model (LLM) chatbot developed by OpenAI. ChatGPT has been trained on a massive dataset of both text and code, giving it the ability to generate code as well as creative text content. Being optimized for conversations, ChatGPT allowed users to steer the conversations to generate the desired content by considering the succeeding prompts and replies as context.

Because of these capabilities and it being made available to the general public, ChatGPT gained immense popularity. It became the fastest-growing consumer software application in history. Since release, it has been covered by major news outlets, reviewed in both technical and nontechnical industries, and even referenced in government documents. The amount of interest shown in ChatGPT by the general public is something previously unheard of. The availability of it has made a substantial impact on many industries both directly and indirectly. This has resulted in both enthusiasm and concerns about AI and its capabilities.

© Thimira Amaratunga 2023
T. Amaratunga, *Understanding Large Language Models*,
https://doi.org/10.1007/979-8-8688-0017-7_1

While being the most popular LLM product, ChatGPT is barely the tip of the iceberg when it comes to the capabilities of large language models. Ushered in by the advancements of deep learning, natural language processing (NLP), and the ever-increasing processing power of data processing, LLMs are the bleeding edge of generative AI. The technology has been in active development since 2018. ChatGPT is not the first LLM. In fact, it was not even the first LLM from OpenAI. It was, however, the most impactful one to reach the general public. The success of ChatGPT has also triggered a wave of competitor conversational AI platforms, such as Bard from Google and LLaMA from Meta AI, pushing the boundaries of the technology further.

As with any new technology, not everyone seems to have grasped what LLMs really are. Also, while many have expressed enthusiasm regarding LLMs and their capabilities, there are concerns being raised. The concerns range from AI taking over certain job roles, disruption of creative processes, forgeries, and existential risk brought on by superintelligent AIs. However, some of these concerns are due to the misunderstanding of LLMs. There are real potential risks associated with LLMs. But it may not be from where most people are thinking.

To understand both the usefulness and the risks, we must first learn how LLMs work and the history of AI that led to the development of LLMs.

A Brief History of AI

Humans have always been intrigued by the idea of intelligent machines: the idea that machines or artificial constructs can be built with intelligent behavior, allowing them to perform tasks that typically require human intelligence. This idea pre-dates the concept of computers, and written records of the idea can be traced back to the 13th century. By the 19th century, it was this idea that brought forward concepts such as formal reasoning, propositional logic, and predicate calculus.

In June 1956, many expert mathematicians and scientists who were enthusiasts in the subject of intelligent machines came together for a conference at Dartmouth College (New Hampshire, US). This conference—The Dartmouth Summer Research Project on Artificial Intelligence—was the starting point of the formal research field of artificial intelligence. It was at this conference that the Logic Theorist, developed by Allen Newell, Herbert A. Simon, and Cliff Shaw and what is now considered to be the first artificial intelligence program, was also presented. The Logic Theorist was meant to mimic the logical problem-solving of a human and was able to prove 38 out of the first 52 theorems in *Principia Mathematica* (a book on the principles of mathematics written by Alfred North Whitehead and Bertrand Russell).

After its initiation, the field of artificial intelligence branched out into several subfields, such as expert systems, computer vision, natural language processing, etc. These subfields often overlap and build upon each other. Over the following years, AI has experienced several waves of optimism, followed by disappointment and the loss of funding (time periods referred to as *AI winters,* which are followed by new approaches being discovered, success, and renewed funding and interest).

One of the main obstacles the researchers of AI faced at the time was the incomplete understanding of intelligence. Even today we lack a complete understanding of how human intelligence works. By the late 1990s, researchers proposed a new approach: rather than attempting to code intelligent behavior into a system, build a system that can grow its own intelligence. This idea created a new subfield of AI named *machine learning*.

The main aim of machine learning (ML) is to provide machines with the ability to learn without explicit programming, in the hopes that such systems once built will be able to evolve and adapt when they are exposed to new data. The core idea is the ability of a learner to generalize from experience. The learner (the AI system being trained), once given a set of training samples, must be able to build a generalized model upon them, which would allow it to decide upon new cases with sufficient accuracy. Such training in ML can be provided in three main methods.

- *Supervised learning*: the system is given a set of labeled cases (training set) based on which the system is asked to create a generalized model that can act on unseen cases.

- *Unsupervised learning*: The system is given a set of unlabeled cases and asked to find a pattern in them. This is ideal for discovering hidden patterns.

- *Reinforcement learning*: The system is asked to take any action and is given a reward or a penalty based on how appropriate that action is to the given situation. The system must learn which actions yield the most rewards in given situations over time.

Machine learning can also use a combination of these main learning methods, such as semi-supervised learning in which a small number of labeled examples are used with a large set of unlabeled data for training.

With these base concepts of machine learning several models were introduced as means of implementing trainable systems and learning techniques, such as artificial neural networks (models inspired by how neurons of the brain work), decision trees (models that use tree-like structures to model decisions and outcomes), regression models (models that use statistical methods to map input and output variables), etc. These models proved exceptionally effective in areas such as computer vision and natural language processing.

The success of machine learning saw a steady growth in AI research and applications over the next decade. By around 2010 few other factors occurred that pushed their progress further.

Building AI models, especially machine learning models such as neural networks, has always been computationally intensive. By the early 2010s computing power started becoming cheaper and more available as more powerful and efficient processors were becoming available. In addition, specialist hardware platforms that benefited AI model training became available. This allowed more complex models to be evaluated. In parallel, the cost of data storage and processing continued to decline. This made collecting and processing large datasets more viable. Finally, advancements in the medical field increased the understanding of how the natural brain works. This new knowledge, and the availability of processing power and data, allowed more complex neural network models to be created and trained.

It was identified that the natural brain uses a hierarchical method to obtain knowledge, by building complicated concepts out of simpler ones. The brain does this by identifying lower-level patterns from the raw inputs and then building upon those patterns to learn higher-level features over many levels. This technique, when modeled on machine learning, is known as *hierarchical feature learning* and allows such systems to automatically learn complex features through multiple levels of abstraction with minimal human intervention. When applying hierarchical feature learning to neural networks, it results in deep networks with many feature learning layers. Thus, this approach was called *deep learning*.

A deep learning model will not try to understand the entire problem at once. Instead, it will look at the input, piece by piece, so that it can derive from its lower-level patterns/features. It then uses these lower-level features to gradually identify higher-level features, through many layers, hierarchically. This allows deep learning models to learn complicated patterns, by gradually building them up from simpler ones, allowing them to comprehend the world better.

Deep learning models were immensely successful in the tasks they were trained on, resulting in many deep learning architectures being developed such as convolutional neural networks (CNNs), stacked autoencoders, generative adversarial networks (GANs), transformers, etc. Their success resulted in deep learning architectures being applied to many other AI fields such as computer vision and natural language processing.

In 2014, with the advancements in models such as variational autoencoders and generative adversarial networks, deep learning models were able to generate new data based on what they learned from their training. With the introduction of the transformer deep learning architecture in 2017, such capabilities were pushed even further. These latest generations of AI models were named *generative AI* and within a few short years were able to generate images, art, music, videos, code, text, and more.

This is where LLMs come into the picture.

Where LLMs Stand

Large language models are the result of the combination of natural language processing, deep learning concepts, and generative AI models. Figure 1-1 shows where LLMs stand in the AI landscape.

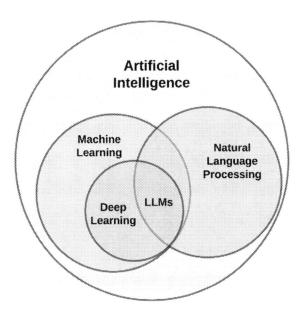

Figure 1-1. *Where LLMs are in the AI landscape*

Summary

In this chapter, we went through the history of AI and how it has evolved. We also looked at where large language models stand in the broader AI landscape. In the next few chapters, we will look at the evolution of NLP and its core concepts, the transformer architecture, and the unique features of LLMs.

CHAPTER 2

NLP Through the Ages

Natural language processing (NLP) is a subfield of artificial intelligence and computational linguistics. It focuses on enabling computers to understand, interpret, and generate human language in a way that is both meaningful and useful. The primary goal of NLP is to bridge the gap between human language and computer understanding, allowing machines to process, analyze, and respond to natural language data.

NLP is the heart of large language models (LLMs). LLMs would not exist without the concepts and algorithms developed through NLP research over the years. Therefore, to understand LLMs, we need to understand the concepts of NLP.

History of NLP

The conception of natural language processing dates to the 1950s. In 1950, Alan Turing published an article titled "Computing Machinery and Intelligence," which discussed a method to determine whether a machine exhibits human-like intelligence. This proposed test, most popularly referred to as the *Turing test*, is widely considered as what inspired early NLP researchers to attempt natural language understanding.

© Thimira Amaratunga 2023
T. Amaratunga, *Understanding Large Language Models*,
https://doi.org/10.1007/979-8-8688-0017-7_2

The Turing test involves a setup where a human evaluator interacts with both a human and a machine without knowing which is which. The evaluator's task is to determine which participant is the machine and which is the human based solely on their responses to questions or prompts. If the machine is successful in convincing the evaluator that it is human, then it is said to have passed the Turing test. The Turing test thus provided a concrete and measurable goal for AI research. Turing's proposal sparked interest and discussions about the possibility of creating intelligent machines that could understand and communicate in natural language like humans. This led to the establishment of NLP as a fundamental research area within AI.

In 1956, with the establishment of the artificial intelligence research field, NLP became an established field of research in AI, making it one of the oldest subfields in AI research.

During the 1960s and 1970s, NLP research predominantly relied on rule-based systems. One of the earliest NLP programs was the ELIZA chatbot, developed by Joseph Weizenbaum between 1964 and 1966. ELIZA used pattern matching and simple rules to simulate conversation between the user and a psychotherapist. With an extremely limited vocabulary and ruleset ELIZA was still able to articulate human-like interactions. The General Problem Solver (GPS) system, developed in the 1970s by Allen Newell and Herbert A. Simon, working with means-end analysis, also demonstrated some language processing capabilities.

In the 1970s and 1980s, NLP research began to incorporate linguistic theories and principles to understand language better. Noam Chomsky's theories on generative grammar and transformational grammar influenced early NLP work. These approaches aimed to use linguistic knowledge and formal grammatical rules to understand and process human language.

The following are some key aspects of linguistic-based approaches in NLP.

Formal Grammars

Linguistics-based NLP heavily relied on formal grammars, such as context-free grammars and phrase structure grammars. These formalisms provided a way to represent the hierarchical structure and rules of natural language sentences.

Transformational Grammar and Generative Grammar

Noam Chomsky's transformational grammar and generative grammar theories significantly influenced early NLP research. These theories focused on the idea that sentences in a language are generated from underlying abstract structures, and rules of transformation govern the relationship between these structures.

Parsing and Syntactic Analysis

Parsing, also known as *syntactic analysis*, was a crucial aspect of linguistics-based NLP. It involved breaking down sentences into their grammatical components and determining the hierarchical structure. Researchers explored various parsing algorithms to analyze the syntax of sentences.

Context and Semantics

Linguistics-based approaches aimed to understand the context and semantics of sentences beyond just their surface structure. The focus was on representing the meaning of words and phrases in a way that allowed systems to reason about their semantic relationships.

Language Understanding

Linguistics-based NLP systems attempted to achieve deeper language understanding by incorporating syntactic and semantic knowledge. This understanding was crucial for more advanced NLP tasks, such as question answering and natural language understanding.

Knowledge Engineering

In many cases, these approaches required manual knowledge engineering, where linguistic rules and structures had to be explicitly defined by human experts. This process was time-consuming and limited the scalability of NLP systems.

There are, however, some limitations in linguistics-based NLP approaches. While linguistics-based approaches had theoretical appeal and offered some insights into language structure, they also faced limitations. The complexity of natural languages and the vast number of exceptions to linguistic rules made it challenging to develop comprehensive and robust NLP systems solely based on formal grammars.

Because of these limitations, while linguistic theories continued to play a role in shaping the NLP field, they were eventually complemented and, in some cases, surpassed by data-driven approaches and statistical methods.

During the 1990s and 2000s, NLP started shifting its focus from rule-based and linguistics-driven systems to data-driven methods. These approaches leveraged large amounts of language data to build probabilistic models, leading to significant advancements in various NLP tasks.

Statistical NLP methods used several approaches and applications. Let us look at a few next.

Probabilistic Models

Statistical approaches relied on probabilistic models to process and analyze language data. These models assigned probabilities to different linguistic phenomena based on their occurrences in large annotated corpora.

Hidden Markov Models

Hidden Markov models (HMMs) were one of the early statistical models used in NLP. They were employed for tasks such as part-of-speech tagging and speech recognition. HMMs use probability distributions to model the transition between hidden states, which represent the underlying linguistic structures.

N-Gram Language Models

N-gram language models became popular during this era. They predicted the likelihood of a word occurring given the preceding (n-1) words. N-grams are simple but effective for tasks such as language modelling, machine translation, and information retrieval.

Maximum Entropy Models

Maximum entropy (MaxEnt) models were widely used in various NLP tasks. They are a flexible probabilistic framework that can incorporate multiple features and constraints to make predictions.

Conditional Random Fields

Conditional random fields (CRFs) gained popularity for sequence labeling tasks, such as part-of-speech tagging and named entity recognition. CRFs model the conditional probabilities of labels given the input features.

Large Annotated Corpora

Statistical approaches relied on large annotated corpora for training and evaluation. These corpora were essential for estimating the probabilities used in probabilistic models and for evaluating the performance of NLP systems.

Word Sense Disambiguation

Statistical methods were applied to word sense disambiguation (WSD) tasks, where the goal was to determine the correct sense of a polysemous word based on context. Supervised and unsupervised methods were explored for this task.

Machine Translation

Statistical machine translation (SMT) systems emerged, which used statistical models to translate text from one language to another. Phrase-based and hierarchical models were common approaches in SMT.

Information Retrieval

Statistical techniques were applied to information retrieval tasks, where documents were ranked based on their relevance to user queries.

While statistical approaches showed great promise, they still faced challenges related to data sparsity, handling long-range dependencies in language, and capturing complex semantic relationships between words.

During the 2000s and 2010s, as we discussed in the history of AI, there was a significant rise in the application of machine learning (ML) techniques. This period witnessed tremendous advancements in ML algorithms, computational power, and the availability of large text corpora, which fueled the progress of NLP research and applications.

Several key developments contributed to the rise of machine learning–based NLP during this time. Let us explore a few of them.

Statistical Approaches

Statistical approaches became dominant in NLP during this period. Instead of hand-crafted rule-based systems, researchers started using probabilistic models and ML algorithms to solve NLP tasks. Techniques like HMMs, CRFs, and support vector machines (SVMs) gained popularity.

Availability of Large Text Corpora

The rise of the Internet and digitalization led to the availability of vast amounts of text data. Researchers could now train ML models on large corpora, which greatly improved the performance of NLP systems.

Supervised Learning for NLP Tasks

Supervised learning became widely used for various NLP tasks. With labeled data for tasks like part-of-speech tagging, named entity recognition (NER), sentiment analysis, and machine translation, researchers could train ML models effectively.

Named Entity Recognition

ML-based NER systems, which identify entities such as the names of people, organizations, and locations in text, became more accurate and widely used. This was crucial for information extraction and text understanding tasks.

Sentiment Analysis

Sentiment analysis or opinion mining gained prominence, driven by the increasing interest in understanding public opinions and sentiments expressed in social media and product reviews.

Machine Translation

Statistical machine translation (SMT) systems, using techniques such as phrase-based models, started to outperform rule-based approaches, leading to significant improvements in translation quality.

Introduction of Word Embeddings

Word embeddings, like Word2Vec and GloVe, revolutionized NLP by providing dense vector representations of words. These embeddings captured semantic relationships between words, improving performance in various NLP tasks.

Deep Learning and Neural Networks

The advent of deep learning and neural networks brought about a paradigm shift in NLP. Models like recurrent neural networks (RNNs), long short-term memory (LSTM), and convolutional neural networks (CNNs) significantly improved performance in sequence-to-sequence tasks, sentiment analysis, and machine translation.

Deployment in Real-World Applications

ML-based NLP systems found practical applications in various industries, such as customer support chatbots, virtual assistants, sentiment analysis tools, and machine translation services.

The combination of statistical methods, large datasets, and the advent of deep learning paved the way for the widespread adoption of ML-based NLP during the 2000s and 2010s.

Toward the end of the 2010s, pre-trained language models like ELMo, Generative Pre-trained Transformer (GPT), and Bidirectional Encoder Representations from Transformers (BERT) emerged. These models were pre-trained on vast amounts of data and fine-tuned for specific NLP tasks, achieving state-of-the-art results in various benchmarks. These developments enabled significant progress in language understanding, text generation, and other NLP tasks, making NLP an essential part of many modern applications and services.

Tasks of NLP

With the primary goal of bridging the gap between human language and computer understanding, over its history, NLP has been applied to several tasks concerning language.

- *Text classification*: Assigning a label or category to a piece of text. For example, classifying emails as spam or not spam, sentiment analysis (identifying the sentiment as positive, negative, or neutral), topic categorization, etc.

- *NER*: Identifying and classifying entities mentioned in the text, such as names of people, organizations, locations, dates, and more.

- *Machine translation*: Automatically translating text from one language to another.

- *Text generation*: Creating human-like text, which could be in the form of chatbots, autogenerated content, or text summarization.

- *Speech recognition*: Converting spoken language into written text.

- *Text summarization*: Automatically generating a concise and coherent summary of a longer text.

- *Question answering*: Providing accurate answers to questions asked in natural language.

- *Language modeling*: Predicting the likelihood of a given sequence of words occurring in a language.

The combination of one or more of these tasks forms the basis of current NLP applications.

Basic Concepts of NLP

To achieve the previously mentioned tasks, NLP employs a set of key concepts. These are some of the most common:

- *Tokenization*: Tokenization is the process of breaking down a text into smaller units, typically words or subwords. These smaller units are called *tokens*, and tokenization is an essential preprocessing step in most NLP tasks.

- *Stopword removal*: Stopwords are common words (e.g., *the*, *is*, *and*) that often appear in a text but carry little semantic meaning. Removing stopwords can help reduce noise and improve computational efficiency.

- *Part-of-speech (POS) tagging*: POS tagging involves assigning grammatical tags (e.g., noun, verb, adjective) to each word in a sentence, indicating its syntactic role.

- *Parsing*: Parsing involves analyzing the grammatical structure of a sentence to understand the relationships between words and phrases. Dependency parsing and constituency parsing are common parsing techniques.

- *Word embeddings*: Word embeddings are dense vector representations of words that capture semantic relationships between words. Word2Vec and GloVe are popular word embedding models.

- *NER*: NER is the process of identifying and classifying named entities mentioned in the text, such as names of people, organizations, locations, dates, etc.

- *Stemming and lemmatization*: Stemming and lemmatization are techniques used to reduce words to their base or root form. For example, *running, runs*, and *ran* might all be stemmed or lemmatized to *run*.

- *Language models*: Language models predict the likelihood of a sequence of words occurring in a language. They play a crucial role in various NLP tasks, such as machine translation and text generation.

Apart from these other task-specific techniques such as sequence-to-sequence models, attention mechanisms and transfer learning mechanisms are also used in NLP.

Let us investigate some of these concepts in depth, which will give us a better understanding of the internal workings of LLMs.

Tokenization

Tokenization is the process of breaking down a text or a sequence of characters into smaller units, called *tokens*. In NLP, tokens are typically words or subwords that form the basic building blocks for language processing tasks. Tokenization is a crucial preprocessing step before text can be used in various NLP applications.

Let's take an example sentence: "I love natural language processing!" The word level tokenization output would be as follows:

```
["I", "love", "natural", "language", "processing", "!"]
```

In this example, the tokenization process splits the sentence into individual words, removing any punctuation. Each word in the sentence becomes a separate token, forming a list of tokens.

Tokenization can be performed using various methods, and the choice of tokenizer depends on the specific NLP task and the characteristics of the text data. Some common tokenization techniques include the following:

- *Whitespace tokenization*: The text is split into tokens based on whitespace (spaces, tabs, newlines). It's a simple and common approach for English text and can handle most cases, but it may not handle special cases like hyphenated words or contractions well.

- *Punctuation tokenization*: The text is split based on punctuation marks, such as periods, commas, exclamation marks, etc. It can be useful when handling text with significant punctuation, but it may result in issues when dealing with abbreviations or other special cases.

- *Word tokenization*: This is a more advanced tokenizer that uses language-specific rules to split text into words. It can handle special cases like hyphenated words, contractions, and punctuation in a more linguistically accurate manner.

- *Subword tokenization*: Subword tokenization methods like byte-pair encoding (BPE) and SentencePiece split words into subword units, allowing the model to handle out-of-vocabulary words and handle rare or unseen words more effectively.

The choice of tokenizer can depend on the specific use case and requirements of the NLP task. Tokenization is the first step in converting raw text into a format that can be processed and analyzed by NLP models and algorithms.

Corpus and Vocabulary

In NLP, a *corpus* refers to a large collection of text documents or utterances that are used as a dataset for language analysis and model training. A corpus serves as the primary source of data for various NLP tasks, allowing researchers and practitioners to study language patterns, extract linguistic information, and develop language models.

A corpus can take various forms depending on the specific NLP task or research objective. Some common types of corpora include the following:

- *Text corpora*: A text corpus is a collection of written text documents, such as books, articles, web pages, emails, and social media posts. Text corpora are commonly used for tasks such as language modeling, sentiment analysis, text classification, and information retrieval.

- *Speech corpora*: A speech corpus consists of audio recordings or transcriptions of spoken language. Speech corpora are used in tasks such as speech recognition, speaker identification, and emotion detection.

- *Parallel corpora*: A parallel corpus contains text in multiple languages that are aligned at the sentence or document level. Parallel corpora are used for machine translation and cross-lingual tasks.

- *Treebanks*: Treebanks are annotated corpora that include syntactic parse trees, representing the grammatical structure of sentences. Treebanks are used in tasks like parsing and syntax-based machine learning.

- *Multimodal corpora*: Multimodal corpora include text along with other modalities, such as images, videos, or audio. They are used in tasks that involve understanding and generating information from multiple modalities.

Building and curating high-quality corpora is essential for the success of various NLP applications, as the performance and generalization of language models heavily rely on the quality and diversity of the data they are trained on.

A vocabulary in NLP refers to the set of unique words or tokens present in a corpus of text. It is a fundamental component of language processing, as it defines the complete list of words that a model or system can understand and work with.

When processing text data, the following steps are typically performed to create a vocabulary:

1. *Tokenization*: The text is split into individual tokens, which can be words, subwords, or characters, depending on the tokenization strategy used.

2. *Filtering and normalization*: Common preprocessing steps such ss converting text to lowercase, removing punctuation, and filtering out stopwords are applied to clean the data and reduce the size of the vocabulary.

3. *Building vocabulary*: After tokenization and preprocessing, the unique tokens in the text data are collected to form the vocabulary. Each token is assigned a unique numerical index, which serves as its representation in the model or during encoding processes.

The vocabulary is often used to create numerical representations of text data. In many NLP models, words are represented as dense vectors (word embeddings) where each word's embedding is indexed using its integer representation in the vocabulary. This allows words to be processed and manipulated as numerical data, making it easier for machine learning models to work with textual information.

The size of the vocabulary depends on the corpus of text used for training the model. Large-scale models, such as LLMs, often have very extensive vocabularies containing hundreds of thousands or even millions of unique words.

Handling the vocabulary size can be a challenge, as very large vocabularies require more memory and computational resources. Techniques like subword tokenization, which splits words into subword units, and methods like Byte-Pair Encoding (BPE) or SentencePiece, can be used to handle large vocabularies more efficiently and handle rare or out-of-vocabulary words.

Word Embeddings

Word embeddings are dense vector representations of words in a continuous vector space, where similar words are closer to each other. These representations capture semantic relationships between words, allowing NLP models to understand word meanings based on their context.

The main advantages of word embeddings are as follows:

- *Semantic meaning*: Word embeddings capture semantic meaning and relationships between words. Similar words are close to each other in the embedding space, and analogies like "man is to woman as king is to queen" can be represented as vector arithmetic.

- *Dimensionality reduction*: Word embeddings reduce the dimensionality of the word representation compared to one-hot encodings. While one-hot encodings are binary vectors with a length equal to the vocabulary size, word embeddings typically have much smaller fixed dimensions (e.g., 100, 300) regardless of the vocabulary size.

- *Generalization*: Word embeddings generalize across words, allowing models to learn from limited data. Words that share similar contexts tend to have similar embeddings, which enables models to understand the meaning of new words based on their context.

- *Continuous space*: The embedding space is continuous, enabling interpolation and exploration of relationships between words. For example, one can add the vector for "Spain" to "capital" and subtract "France" to find a vector close to "Madrid."

Word embeddings are a fundamental tool in NLP and have greatly improved the performance of various NLP tasks, such as machine translation, sentiment analysis, text classification, and information retrieval. Popular word embedding methods include simpler methods such as bag-of-words (BoW) to more sophisticated methods such as Word2Vec, Global Vectors for Word Representation (GloVe), and fastText. These methods learn word embeddings by considering the co-occurrence patterns of words in large text corpora, allowing the representations to capture the semantic meaning and contextual relationships of words in the language.

Let us investigate two of these methods, bag-of-words and Word2Vec, in more detail.

Bag-of-Words

The BoW method is a simple and popular technique for text representation. It disregards the order and structure of words in a document and focuses on the frequency of each word in the text. The BoW model represents a document as a histogram of word occurrences, creating a "bag" of words without considering their sequence.

Here are the steps of the bag-of-words method:

1. *Tokenization*: The first step is to break down the text into individual words or tokens.

2. *Vocabulary creation*: The BoW model creates a vocabulary, which is a list of all unique words found in the corpus. Each word in the vocabulary is assigned a unique index.

3. *Vectorization*: To represent a document using BoW, a vector is created for each document, with the length equal to the size of the vocabulary. Each element of the vector corresponds to a word in the vocabulary, and its value represents the frequency of that word in the document.

25

Here is an example on the bag-of-words method:

Let us take a corpus of the following three sentences:

- "I love to eat pizza."

- "She enjoys eating pasta."

- "They like to cook burgers."

Step 1: Tokenization

The tokens in the corpus are: ["I", "love", "to", "eat", "pizza", "She", "enjoys", "eating", "pasta", "They", "like", "to", "cook", "burgers"].

Step 2: Vocabulary Creation

The vocabulary contains all unique words from the tokenized corpus: ["I", "love", "to", "eat", "pizza", "She", "enjoys", "eating", "pasta", "They", "like", "cook", "burgers"].

The vocabulary size is 13.

Step 3: Vectorization

Now, each document is represented as a vector using the vocabulary. The vectors for the three sentences will be as follows:

[1, 1, 1, 1, 1, 0, 0, 0, 0, 0, 0, 0, 0]

(The vector shows that the words *I, love, to, eat,* and *pizza* appear once in the document.)

[0, 0, 0, 1, 0, 1, 1, 1, 1, 0, 0, 0, 0]

(The vector shows that the words *She, enjoys, eating,* and *pasta* appear once in the document.)

[0, 0, 1, 0, 0, 0, 0, 0, 0, 1, 1, 1, 1]

(The vector shows that the words *They, like, to, cook,* and *burgers* appear once in the document.)

Note that the order of the words is lost in the BoW representation, and each document is represented solely based on the frequency of the words present in it.

The BoW method is a straightforward and effective way to convert text into numerical vectors for use in various machine learning algorithms and NLP tasks, such as text classification and information retrieval. However, it does not consider the context or semantics of words, which can limit its ability to capture deeper meaning in language data.

Word2Vec

Word2Vec is a popular and influential word embedding method in NLP. It was introduced by Tomas Mikolov et al. at Google in 2013 and has since become a foundational technique in various NLP tasks. The main idea behind Word2Vec is to represent words as points in a high-dimensional space, where the relative positions of words capture their semantic relationships and contextual similarities. Words that appear in similar contexts or have similar meanings are mapped to vectors that are close to each other in the embedding space.

There are two primary architectures for training Word2Vec models.

- *Continuous bag-of-words (CBOW)*

    CBOW aims to predict the target word given its context (surrounding words). It uses a neural network to learn word embeddings by taking the context words as input and predicting the target word.

    The context words are represented as one-hot-encoded vectors or embeddings, and they are averaged to form a single context vector.

    The CBOW model tries to minimize the prediction error between the predicted target word and the actual target word.

- *Skip-gram*

  Skip-gram, on the other hand, aims to predict the context words given a target word. It tries to learn the embeddings by maximizing the likelihood of the context words given the target word.

  The target word is represented as a one-hot-encoded vector or embedding, and the model tries to predict the surrounding context words based on this representation.

  Skip-gram is often preferred when the dataset is large, as it generates more training examples by considering all the context words for each target word.

During training, Word2Vec uses a shallow neural network to learn the embeddings. The weights of the neural network are updated during the training process using stochastic gradient descent or similar optimization techniques. The objective is to learn word embeddings that effectively capture the word semantics and co-occurrence patterns in the corpus.

Once trained, the Word2Vec model provides word embeddings that can be used as input to various NLP tasks or serve as a powerful representation for downstream applications. The trained embeddings can be used in tasks such as sentiment analysis, machine translation, document classification, and information retrieval, where they capture the meaning and relationships between words in a continuous vector space. Word2Vec has been instrumental in advancing the performance of NLP models by enabling them to work effectively with textual data in a more semantically meaningful manner.

The typical process to train a Word2Vec model would involve the following steps:

1. *Data preparation*:

   Gather a large corpus of text data that will be used for training the Word2Vec model. The corpus should represent the domain or language you want to capture word embeddings for.

2. *Tokenization*:

   Tokenize the text data to break it down into individual words or subwords. Remove any unwanted characters, punctuation, and stopwords during tokenization.

3. *Create context-target pairs*:

   For each target word in the corpus, create context-target pairs. The context is a window of words surrounding the target word. The size of the window is a hyperparameter, typically set to a small value like 5 to 10 words. The context-target pairs are used to train the model to predict the context given the target word, or vice versa.

4. *Convert words to indices*:

   Convert the words in the context-target pairs into numerical indices, as Word2Vec models typically work with integer word indices rather than actual word strings.

5. *Create training examples*:

    Use the context-target pairs to create training
    examples for the Word2Vec model. Each training
    example consists of a target word (input) and its
    corresponding context words (output) or vice
    versa, depending on the architecture (CBOW or
    skip-gram).

6. *Architecture selection*:

    Choose the architecture you want to use for the
    Word2Vec model. The two main architectures are
    the following:

    - *CBOW*: Predict the target word based on the
      context words.

    - *Skip-gram*: Predict the context words based on
      the target word.

7. *Define the neural network*:

    Create a shallow neural network for the chosen
    architecture. The network will consist of an
    embedding layer that represents words as dense
    vectors and a softmax layer (for CBOW) or negative
    sampling (for skip-gram) to perform the word
    predictions.

8. *Training*:

    Train the Word2Vec model on the training
    examples using stochastic gradient descent or other
    optimization algorithms. The objective is to minimize
    the prediction loss, which measures the difference
    between predicted and actual context or target words.

9. *Learn word embeddings*:

   As the model trains, the embedding layer learns to map each word to a dense vector representation. These word embeddings capture semantic relationships and meaning based on the co-occurrence patterns of words in the corpus.

10. *Evaluation*:

    After training, evaluate the quality of the learned word embeddings on downstream NLP tasks, such as word similarity, analogies, or text classification, to ensure they capture meaningful semantic information.

The training process may require hyperparameter tuning, and the model may need to be trained on a large corpus and for multiple epochs to learn effective word embeddings. Once trained, the Word2Vec model can be used to generate word vectors for any word in the vocabulary, enabling the exploration of semantic relationships between words in a continuous vector space.

Because of the popularity of the Word2Vec model, many machine learning and NLP libraries have built-in implementations of it. This allows you to easily utilize Word2Vec embeddings in your code without having to manually train neural networks for it.

Bag-of-Words vs. Word2Vec

While both Bag-of-Words and Word2Vec are text representation methods in NLP there are some key differences between them.

Representation

- *Bag-of-Words (BoW)*: BoW represents a document as a histogram of word occurrences, without considering the order or structure of the words. It creates a "bag" of words, and each element in the vector represents the frequency of a specific word in the document.

- *Word2Vec*: Word2Vec, on the other hand, represents words as dense vectors in a continuous vector space. It captures the semantic meaning and relationships between words based on their context in the corpus. Word2Vec embeddings are learned through a shallow neural network model trained on a large dataset.

Context and semantics

- *BoW*: BoW does not consider the context or semantics of words in a document. It treats each word as an independent entity and focuses only on the frequency of occurrence.

- *Word2Vec*: Word2Vec leverages the distributional hypothesis, which suggests that words with similar meanings tend to appear in similar contexts. Word2Vec captures word embeddings that encode semantic relationships, allowing for better understanding of word meanings and similarities based on context.

Vector size

- *BoW*: The size of the BoW vector is equal to the size of the vocabulary in the corpus. Each word in the vocabulary is represented by a unique index, and the vector elements indicate the frequency of occurrence.

- *Word2Vec*: Word2Vec generates dense word embeddings, typically with a fixed size (e.g., 100, 300 dimensions). The size of the word embeddings is generally much smaller compared to the BoW vector, which can be useful for memory and computational efficiency.

Order of words

- *BoW*: BoW ignores the order of words in the document, as it treats each document as a collection of individual words and their frequencies. The order of words is lost in the BoW representation.

- *Word2Vec*: Word2Vec considers the order of words in the context window during training. It learns word embeddings by predicting the likelihood of words appearing in the context of other words, which allows it to capture word meanings based on the surrounding words.

Application

- *BoW*: BoW is commonly used for text classification, sentiment analysis, and information retrieval tasks. It is a simple and effective representation for these tasks, especially when the sequence of words is not crucial.

- *Word2Vec*: Word2Vec is more suitable for tasks that require understanding word semantics and capturing word relationships, such as word similarity, word analogies, and language generation tasks.

In summary, bag-of-words is a straightforward and interpretable method that represents text using word frequencies but lacks contextual understanding. Word2Vec, on the other hand, generates dense word embeddings that capture semantic meaning and relationships between words based on context, making it more suitable for various advanced NLP tasks.

Language Modeling

In natural language processing, language models are a class of models that are designed to predict the likelihood of a sequence of words occurring in a language. In other words, A language model is a probability distribution over sequences of words. These models learn the statistical properties and patterns present in a given language to generate new text or evaluate the likelihood of a sentence.

Language models play a crucial role in various NLP tasks, such as machine translation, speech recognition, text generation, sentiment analysis, and more. They are fundamental to many advanced NLP applications such as LLMs and have contributed significantly to the success of modern NLP techniques.

Based on the tasks they perform language models can be broadly classify into two categories:

- *Generative language models*: These models are designed to generate new text based on the patterns they have learned from the training data. They take a seed input (known as a *prompt* or *starting sequence*) and then generate the next word or sequence of words one step at a time. Generative language models can be used for tasks like text generation, story generation, and poetry writing.

- *Predictive language models*: These models are used to predict the likelihood of the next word in a given context. They take the previous words as input and predict the most probable next word based on the training data. Predictive language models are widely used in tasks like autocomplete, next-word prediction, and machine translation.

Based on their approach, there are primarily two types of language models:

- *N-gram language models*: N-gram language models are the simplest form. They predict the probability of a word based on the occurrence of the previous (n-1) words in the text. The "n" in n-gram refers to the number of words in the sequence. For example, a 2-gram (bigram) language model predicts the probability of a word based on the previous word, and a 3-gram (trigram) language model considers the two preceding words.

  Example (2-gram model):

  Sentence: "I love to"

  Probability of "to" given "I love": $P(to \mid I\ love)$

  N-gram models have limitations in capturing long-range dependencies and contextual information, as they consider only a fixed number of preceding words.

- *Neural language models*: Neural language models, also known as *neural network–based language models*, are more advanced and widely used in modern NLP. These models use deep learning techniques to learn word representations and capture complex relationships between words in a more flexible manner.

- *Recurrent neural networks (RNNs)*: RNNs are one of the earliest neural language models that can consider variable-length context. They use a recurrent architecture to process words sequentially while maintaining a hidden state that captures the context.

- *Long short-term memory (LSTM) and gated recurrent units (GRUs)*: These are variations of RNNs designed to address the vanishing gradient problem, allowing them to capture long-range dependencies more effectively.

- *Transformers*: Transformers have revolutionized the field of NLP and are the basis for many state-of-the-art language models. Transformers utilize self-attention mechanisms to process words in parallel, capturing both short and long-range dependencies efficiently. LLMs like Generative Pre-trained Transformer (GPT) and Bidirectional Encoder Representations from Transformers (BERT) are examples of successful transformer-based language models.

Let us investigate each of the approaches to language models.

N-Gram Language Models

N-gram language models are a class of statistical language models used in NLP to predict the likelihood of a sequence of words (n-grams) occurring in a given text. These models are based on the principle of conditional probability, where the probability of a word is estimated based on the context of the preceding words.

In an N-gram language model, an "N-gram" refers to a contiguous sequence of N words from a text. For example:

- *Unigram (1-gram)*: Single words in isolation

- *Bigram (2-gram)*: Pairs of consecutive words

- *Trigram (3-gram)*: Triplets of consecutive words

- *N-gram*: A sequence of N consecutive words

The primary idea behind N-gram language models is to approximate the probability of a word given its N-1 preceding words, as shown by the following formula:

```
P(w_i | w_1, w_2, ..., w_{i-1}) ≈ Count(w_{i-N+1}, w_{i-N+2},
..., w_{i-1}, w_i) / Count(w_{i-N+1}, w_{i-N+2}, ..., w_{i-1})
```

where:

- `P(w_i | w_1, w_2, ..., w_{i-1})` is the probability of word `w_i` given the context of the preceding words `w_1, w_2, ..., w_{i-1}`.

- `Count(w_{i-N+1}, w_{i-N+2}, ..., w_{i-1}, w_i)` is the count of the N-gram (sequence) `w_{i-N+1}, w_{i-N+2}, ..., w_{i-1}, w_i` in the training data.

- `Count(w_{i-N+1}, w_{i-N+2}, ..., w_{i-1})` is the count of the (N-1)-gram (sequence) `w_{i-N+1}, w_{i-N+2}, ..., w_{i-1}` in the training data.

In practice, to compute these probabilities, a large corpus of text is used as the training data. The model builds a frequency table of all observed N-grams in the training data, and the probabilities are estimated by dividing the count of the N-gram by the count of its context.

The main steps in building and using an N-gram language model are as follows:

1. Collect and preprocess a large corpus of text for training.

2. Tokenize the text into words or subwords.

3. Build a frequency table of N-grams and their counts in the training data.

4. Estimate the probabilities of N-grams using the frequency table.

5. Use the N-gram probabilities to predict the next word in a given context or to generate new text.

Let us take an example for building an n-gram language model using lyrics from the song "Imagine" by John Lennon:

```
"Imagine there's no heaven
It's easy if you try
No hell below us
Above us only sky
Imagine all the people
Living for today
Ah..."
```

- *Step 1*: Preprocess and tokenize

  ```
  imagine, there's, no, heaven
  it's, easy, if, you, try
  no, hell, below, us
  above, us, only, sky
  imagine, all, the, people
  living, for, today
  ah
  ```

- *Step 2*: Building the N-grams

  ```
  Here, bigrams (2-grams) are considered for
  simplicity.
  ["imagine", "there's"], ["there's", "no"], ["no",
  "heaven"]
  ["it's", "easy"], ["easy", "if"], ["if", "you"],
  ["you", "try"]
  ["no", "hell"], ["hell", "below"],
  ["below", "us"]
  ["above", "us"], ["us", "only"], ["only", "sky"]
  ["imagine", "all"], ["all", "the"], ["the",
  "people"]
  ["living", "for"], ["for", "today"]
  ```

- *Step 3*: Calculating the probabilities

- We can do this by counting the occurrences of
  each bigram.

  ```
  ["imagine", "there's"]: 2 times
  ["there's", "no"]: 1 time
  ["no", "heaven"]: 1 time
  ["it's", "easy"]: 1 time
  ["easy", "if"]: 1 time
  ["if", "you"]: 1 time
  ["you", "try"]: 1 time
  ["no", "hell"]: 1 time
  ["hell", "below"]: 1 time
  ["below", "us"]: 1 time
  ["above", "us"]: 1 time
  ["us", "only"]: 1 time
  ["only", "sky"]: 1 time
  ```

```
["imagine", "all"]: 1 time
["all", "the"]: 1 time
["the", "people"]: 1 time
["living", "for"]: 1 time
["for", "today"]: 1 time
```

- Then calculate the probability of each based on the occurrences.

```
P("imagine" | "there's"): 2/2 = 1.0
P("there's" | "no"): 1/1 = 1.0
P("no" | "heaven"): 1/1 = 1.0
P("it's" | "easy"): 1/1 = 1.0
...
```

Once the bigram probabilities are calculated, they can be used to generate new text.

For example, start with the seed phrase "Imagine there's."

```
P("imagine" | "there's") = 1.0
Predicted next word: "no"
New phrase: "Imagine there's no"

New Seed phrase: "Imagine there's no"
P("there's" | "no") = 1.0
Predicted next word: "heaven"
New phrase: "Imagine there's no heaven"

New Seed phrase: "Imagine there's no heaven"
P("no" | "heaven") = 1.0
Predicted next word: "it's"
New phrase: "Imagine there's no heaven it's"
```

We can continue running the new phrase through the model again and again to get more and more predictions. In practice, higher-order n-grams (e.g., trigrams or higher) may be used to improve text generation quality. This example illustrates just the basic concept of building an n-gram language model using song lyrics as input.

Handling Unknown N-Grams

In the previous example, all bigrams have occurred in the training data, but in a real-world scenario, you may encounter unseen bigrams. To handle this, you can use techniques such as smoothing to assign a small probability to unseen bigrams.

Smoothing, also known as *add-one smoothing* or *Laplace smoothing*, is a technique used to address the issue of zero probabilities for unseen n-grams in language modeling. In an n-gram language model, when an n-gram is encountered in the test data that was not present in the training data, the probability of that n-gram becomes zero in the model. This can lead to unreliable and unrealistic predictions when generating text.

Smoothing addresses this problem by adding a small constant value (usually 1) to the count of all n-grams in the training data before calculating their probabilities. This ensures that even unseen n-grams receive a nonzero probability, and it prevents the model from assigning absolute zero probabilities to any possible sequence of words.

To illustrate smoothing, let us look back at the previous example:

```
["imagine", "there's"]: 2 times
["there's", "no"]: 1 time
["no", "heaven"]: 1 time
["it's", "easy"]: 1 time
["easy", "if"]: 1 time
```

Here it is without smoothing:

```
P("there's" | "no") = 1/1 = 1.0
P("no" | "heaven") = 1/1 = 1.0
```

In this case, the probabilities for "there's" given "no" and "no" given "heaven" are 1.0, which seems reasonable based on the training data. However, if we encounter a new bigram in the test data, such as ["no", "worries"], the probability for this unseen bigram will be zero since it was not in the training data.

Let's look at it with smoothing (add-one smoothing).

Apply add-one smoothing by adding 1 to all bigram counts:

```
["imagine", "there's"]: 3 times (original count + 1)
["there's", "no"]: 2 times (original count + 1)
["no", "heaven"]: 2 times (original count + 1)
["it's", "easy"]: 2 times (original count + 1)
["easy", "if"]: 2 times (original count + 1)
["no", "worries"]: 1 time (unseen bigram, now has a
non-zero count)

P("there's" | "no") = 2/2 = 1.0
P("no" | "heaven") = 2/2 = 1.0
P("no" | "worries") = 1/2 = 0.5 (with add-one smoothing)
```

By applying add-one smoothing, the probabilities for unseen n-grams are no longer zero, and they receive a small probability value. This makes the model more robust and prevents it from being overly confident about the probabilities of unseen n-grams.

Smoothing is a widely used technique in language modeling, especially with small training datasets or when dealing with higher-order n-grams, where the likelihood of unseen n-grams becomes more prevalent.

N-gram language models are relatively simple to implement and can provide reasonable results, especially for lower-order N-grams (e.g., bigrams or trigrams). However, they have limitations when it comes to capturing long-range dependencies and understanding the context beyond a fixed window of N words. To address these limitations, more advanced models like neural language models have been developed, which can capture longer dependencies and generate more coherent and contextually accurate text. Nonetheless, N-gram models remain an essential concept in NLP and have been used in various applications, including text generation, spell checking, speech recognition, and machine translation.

Neural Language Models

Neural language models are a class of advanced language models used in NLP that leverage neural networks to learn the statistical patterns and relationships between words in a large corpus of text. Unlike traditional N-gram models that have limited context and struggle with capturing long-range dependencies, neural language models can process sequences of words with variable length, making them more effective in understanding the context and generating coherent and contextually relevant text.

Neural language models are typically based on two main architectures: recurrent neural networks and transformer-based models.

Recurrent Neural Networks

RNNs are a type of neural network designed to handle sequential data, making them well-suited for processing sequences of words in natural language. RNNs have a recurrent structure that allows them to maintain hidden states, capturing information about the context of previous words. This context is crucial in language modeling, where the meaning of a word often depends on the words that precede it. One of the most widely used RNN variants in language modeling is the long short-term memory (LSTM) network, which is designed to address the vanishing gradient problem and handle long-range dependencies.

Transformer-Based Models

Transformers are a revolutionary architecture introduced in the paper "Attention Is All You Need" by Vaswani et al. in 2017. Transformers employ self-attention mechanisms to capture dependencies between all words in a sequence simultaneously, enabling them to process long-range dependencies more effectively than RNNs. The transformer architecture has become the foundation for many state-of-the-art language models, including the widely known BERT and GPT models.

The training process for neural language models typically involves feeding the model with sequences of words and training it to predict the next word in a sequence given the preceding words. The model's weights are updated during training using backpropagation and gradient descent to minimize the prediction error. The trained model can then be used for various NLP tasks, including text generation, machine translation, sentiment analysis, question-answering, and more.

Recurrent neural networks (RNNs) are bi-directional artificial neural networks, allowing the output from some nodes to affect subsequent input to the same nodes. Their ability to use internal state (memory) to process arbitrary sequences of inputs makes them particularly well-suited for sequential data, making them effective in capturing the temporal dependencies and context in natural language.

The main idea behind RNNs is that they maintain hidden states, which act as memory, to capture information from previous time steps and pass it along to the next time step. This property enables RNNs to handle sequences of variable length and maintain context as they process each word in a sentence.

Typical workings of an RNN-based language model include the following:

- *Word embeddings*: The word embeddings used for RNNs must capture the semantic meaning of words and help the model understand the relationships between different words. Therefore, methods like Word2Vec are used.

- *Sequence processing*: The word embeddings are fed into the RNN one word at a time in a sequential manner. At each time step, the RNN takes the current word embedding and the hidden state from the previous time step as inputs and produces an output and an updated hidden state.

- *Hidden states*: The hidden state at each time step is updated based on the current word embedding and the previous hidden state, allowing the RNN to remember relevant information from previous words.

- *Training*: During training, the RNN is fed with sequences of words from a large corpus of text, and it is trained to minimize the prediction error between the predicted next word and the actual next word in the sequence. The training process uses backpropagation and gradient descent to update the model's parameters and optimize its performance.

- *Prediction*: The output at each time step can be used to predict the probability distribution over the next word in the sequence. By using the output and hidden state at each time step, the model can predict the next word given the preceding words.

RNN-based language models have the advantage of capturing long-range dependencies in sequences, making them effective in understanding the context of words in a sentence. However, they also suffer from some limitations, such as the vanishing gradient problem, which hinders their ability to capture long-term dependencies effectively.

The vanishing gradient problem is a challenge that arises during the training of RNNs, especially those with many layers or long sequences. It occurs due to the nature of the backpropagation algorithm, which is used to update the model's weights during training.

In RNNs, the same set of weights is shared across all time steps, allowing the model to maintain memory of past information and capture sequential dependencies. When processing long sequences, however, the gradients (partial derivatives of the loss with respect to the model's parameters) can become extremely small as they are repeatedly multiplied together during backpropagation.

As the gradients become very small, the updates to the model's weights during training become negligible. Consequently, the RNN struggles to learn long-term dependencies and may fail to capture relevant information from the distant past. This results in the RNN being unable to retain meaningful context beyond a few time steps, limiting its effectiveness in capturing long-range dependencies in the input sequences.

The vanishing gradient problem is particularly problematic in deep RNNs (those with many layers) or when processing sequences of considerable length. When the gradients vanish, the model's learning process slows down significantly, and it may even get stuck in a state where it fails to make any meaningful progress.

To address this issue, various RNN variants with specialized architectures have been introduced, such as the long short-term memory (LSTM) and gated recurrent unit (GRU).

LSTM and GRU architectures include gating mechanisms that selectively control the flow of information through the network. These gating mechanisms help RNNs retain and update relevant information over longer time scales, effectively mitigating the vanishing gradient problem and improving the model's ability to learn long-term dependencies in sequential data.

LSTM-based language models are a variant of RNNs. LSTMs use gating mechanisms to selectively retain and update information in their hidden states, making them more capable of maintaining relevant context over longer sequences.

The basic concepts of LSTM-based language models are as follows:

- *LSTM structure*:

  The LSTM cell is the fundamental building block of the LSTM-based language model. It consists of several components, including the input gate, forget gate, output gate, and cell state.

- *Cell state and hidden state*:

  The LSTM maintains two primary states: the cell state (often denoted as 'c') and the hidden state (often denoted as 'h').

  The cell state is responsible for capturing long-term dependencies in the input sequence. It acts as a memory that stores relevant information from previous time steps.

  The hidden state contains the relevant context for the current time step and is used for making predictions.

- *Gating mechanisms*:

  LSTMs use gating mechanisms to control the flow of information through the cell state. These gates are sigmoid-activated neural networks that produce values between 0 and 1.

The input gate determines how much of the new information should be added to the cell state at the current time step.

The forget gate determines how much of the previous cell state should be retained and carried over to the current time step.

The output gate determines how much of the cell state should be exposed to the next time step as the hidden state.

- *LSTM computation*:

  At each time step, the LSTM cell takes the current word embedding and the previous hidden state as inputs.

  It then computes the values of the input gate, forget gate, and output gate using sigmoid activation functions based on the inputs and the previous hidden state.

  The cell state is updated by combining the output of the forget gate (to forget irrelevant information) and the output of the input gate (to add new relevant information).

  The updated cell state is then used to compute the new hidden state, which becomes the output of the LSTM cell at the current time step.

  The LSTM cell's output (hidden state) is then used to predict the probability distribution over the next word in the sequence.

- *Training and generation*:

  During training, the LSTM-based language model is fed with sequences of words from a large corpus of text and is trained to minimize the prediction error between the predicted next word and the actual next word in the sequence.

  Once the LSTM-based language model is trained, it can be used to generate new text or complete existing text by predicting the next word given a seed input, similar to the standard RNN-based language models.

  LSTM-based language models have shown significant improvements in handling long-range dependencies and capturing context in sequential data. They have become a standard architecture in various NLP tasks.

  GRU-based language models are another variant of RNNs that address the vanishing gradient problem. GRUs use gating mechanisms to selectively control the flow of information through the hidden state, making them effective in retaining relevant context over longer sequences.

The following are the basic concepts of GRU-based language models:

- *GRU structure*:

  The GRU cell is the fundamental building block of the GRU-based language model. It is similar to the LSTM cell but has a simplified structure with fewer parameters.

  The GRU cell consists of several components, including the reset gate and update gate.

- *Hidden state*:

  Similar to LSTM-based language models, the GRU maintains a hidden state (often denoted as 'h'a).

  The hidden state contains the relevant context for the current time step and is used for making predictions.

- *Gating mechanisms*:

  GRUs use two gating mechanisms: the reset gate and the update gate. These gates are sigmoid-activated neural networks that produce values between 0 and 1.

  The reset gate determines how much of the previous hidden state should be forgotten or reset, allowing the GRU to selectively update the hidden state based on the current input and the previous hidden state.

  The update gate determines how much of the new information should be retained and merged into the hidden state.

- *GRU computation*:

  At each time step, the GRU cell takes the current word embedding and the previous hidden state as inputs.

  It computes the values of the reset gate and update gate using sigmoid activation functions based on the inputs and the previous hidden state.

  The GRU then computes the candidate activation, which is a new proposed hidden state that incorporates information from the current input and the reset gate's output.

The candidate activation is combined with the previous hidden state, weighted by the update gate's output, to compute the new hidden state at the current time step.

The GRU cell's output (hidden state) is then used to predict the probability distribution over the next word in the sequence.

- *Training and generation*:

  During training, the GRU-based language model is fed with sequences of words from a large corpus of text and is trained to minimize the prediction error between the predicted next word and the actual next word in the sequence.

  Once the GRU-based language model is trained, it can be used to generate new text or complete existing text by predicting the next word given a seed input, similar to other RNN-based language models.

GRU-based language models have shown excellent performance in capturing long-range dependencies and context in sequential data. They have become popular alternatives to LSTM-based models due to their simpler architecture and efficient training process.

While they share some similarities, LSTMs and GRUs have key differences in their architecture and functionality:

Architecture complexity

- *LSTM*: LSTM has a more complex architecture compared to GRU. It includes three gating mechanisms: the input gate, forget gate, and output gate. These gates control the flow of information and decide what to remember, forget, or output at each time step.

- *GRU*: GRU has a simpler architecture compared to LSTM. It includes only two gating mechanisms: the reset gate and the update gate. These gates allow the GRU to selectively update and retain information in the hidden state.

Number of parameters

- *LSTM*: Because of its more complex architecture with three gating mechanisms, LSTM generally has more parameters compared to GRU.

- *GRU*: GRU has fewer parameters compared to LSTM due to its simpler architecture with two gating mechanisms.

Gate interactions

- *LSTM*: In LSTM, the input gate, forget gate, and output gate interact with each other separately, allowing the model to independently control the flow of information through each gate.

- *GRU*: In GRU, the reset gate and update gate interact with each other in a more integrated manner. The update gate acts as a combination of the input gate and forget gate in LSTM, controlling both updating and forgetting.

Handling long-term dependencies

- *LSTM*: LSTM is explicitly designed to capture long-term dependencies in sequential data. Its architecture with the input, forget, and output gates allows it to retain relevant information in the cell state for longer periods.

- *GRU*: GRU is also effective in handling long-term dependencies but has a simpler gating mechanism, which may make it more efficient and easier to train in some cases.

Computation efficiency

- *GRU*: Because of its simpler architecture and fewer parameters, GRU may be computationally more efficient compared to LSTM. This makes GRU a preferred choice in scenarios where computational resources are limited.

LSTM and GRU are both effective in addressing the vanishing gradient problem and capturing long-term dependencies in sequential data. LSTM's complex architecture with three gating mechanisms provides a more fine-grained control over information flow, making it suitable for tasks requiring precise memory management. On the other hand, GRU's simpler architecture and fewer parameters make it an efficient alternative to LSTM, especially when computational resources are limited. The choice between LSTM and GRU depends on the specific task, available resources, and the trade-off between complexity and performance.

Summary

In this chapter, we discussed the evolution of natural language processing and how different approaches—linguistic-based, statistical, machine learning-based—were applied for language modeling over the years. We also talked about some of the core concepts of NLP such as tokenization, word embeddings, and n-grams. Finally, we looked at RNN-based language models and the advantages they provide.

While RNN-based language models have made significant contributions to NLP tasks, they have been partly surpassed by more recent architectures like transformers. Transformers, especially those used in models like BERT and GPT, have shown superior performance in capturing long-range dependencies and have become the de facto standard for many NLP tasks.

Transformers are the topic of our next chapter.

CHAPTER 3

Transformers

In 2017, Ashish Vaswani et al. from Google Brain and Google Research proposed a revolutionary new architecture of neural networks for natural language processing (NLP) and other sequence-to-sequence tasks in their "Attention Is All You Need" paper. In this paper, Vaswani et al. presented a new approach that relies heavily on attention mechanisms to process sequences, allowing for parallelization, efficient training, and the ability to capture long-range dependencies in data.

This new architecture proved extremely effective and efficient to train, resulting in transformers having effectively replaced other approaches, such as RNNs and LSTMs, after their introduction.

At the core of the transformer architecture, and the key to its efficiency, is the attention mechanism. Therefore, let us look into how attention works.

Paying Attention

In terms of neural networks and deep learning, *attention* is a mechanism that allows a model to focus on—or "pay attention to"—specific parts of the input data while processing it. It is inspired by the human cognitive process of selectively concentrating on certain elements of sensory information while ignoring others. Attention has proven to be a powerful tool in various tasks, particularly in NLP and computer vision.

© Thimira Amaratunga 2023
T. Amaratunga, *Understanding Large Language Models*,
https://doi.org/10.1007/979-8-8688-0017-7_3

The initial idea of attention mechanisms dates back to the early machine learning concepts of the 1990s and has its origins in cognitive psychology and neuroscience, where researchers studied how humans selectively focus on specific information while processing sensory input and how that behavior can be utilized in machine learning models.

One of the notable early works that utilized attention mechanisms was the work "Neural Turing Machine" by Graves et al. (2014), which introduced a differentiable memory addressing mechanism that allows neural networks to access external memory using attention. An application of attention used with computer vision was shown by Xu et al. in "Show, Attend and Tell: Neural Image Caption Generation with Visual Attention" in 2015, which used attention to improve image captioning by focusing on different parts of an image while generating each word of the caption.

Attention mechanisms gained prominence with the development of sequence-to-sequence models. In tasks such as machine translation, the model needs to capture long-range dependencies between the input and output sequences. "Neural Machine Translation by Jointly Learning to Align and Translate" by Bahdanau et al. (2015) introduced the attention mechanism in the context of machine translation. This attention mechanism allowed the model to align different parts of the source and target sentences.

In 2017, Vaswani et al., in their "Attention Is All You Need" paper, further improved the concept by introducing self-attention, scaled dot product, and multihead attention mechanisms.

The attention mechanism works by enabling the model to focus on the most relevant information while generating the output by assigning different weights to different parts of the input sequence. Figure 3-1 shows a visualization of an example of learned dependencies from an attention module of a transformer model.

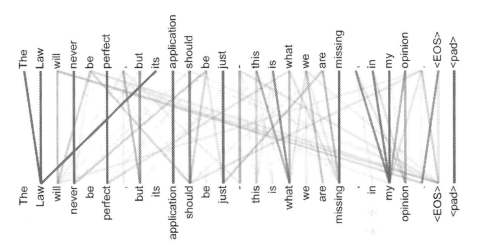

Figure 3-1. *A visualization of an example learned dependencies from an attention module of a transformer model. Source: "Attention Is All You Need" by Vaswani et al.*

These long-distance relationships learned during the training phase allow the model to focus on what is important in a sequence as well as predict the next element in a sequence. Figure 3-2 shows a visualization of how next-word dependencies can be derived.

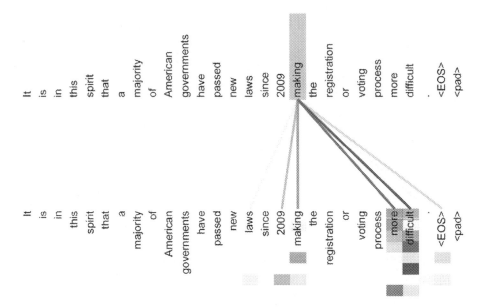

Figure 3-2. *A visualization of how next-word dependencies can be derived. Source: "Attention Is All You Need" by Vaswani et al.*

The typical attention mechanism has three main components: the queries (Q), keys (K), and values (V).

Query (Q)

- The query vector represents the current element for which attention is being computed.

- It is a learned vector that captures the properties or features of the current element.

Key (K)

- The key vectors represent other elements in the sequence.

- They are also learned vectors that encode the properties or features of these other elements.

Value (V)

- The value vectors hold information or content associated with each element in the sequence.

- They are used to compute the weighted sum of values based on attention scores.

To build the attention scores, the following functions are applied to the components.

Attention scores

- Attention scores quantify the relevance or similarity between the Query vector and the Key vectors.

- They are typically computed using the dot product between the Query and Key vectors.

Softmax function

- The softmax function is applied to the attention scores to obtain attention weights.

- The softmax operation converts the scores into a probability distribution, ensuring that the weights sum up to 1.

Weighted sum (context vector)

- The attention weights obtained from the softmax operation are used to compute a weighted sum of the Value vectors.

- The weighted sum is the context vector, which captures the contribution of each element to the current element's representation.

Figure 3-3 illustrates a simplified view of this workflow.

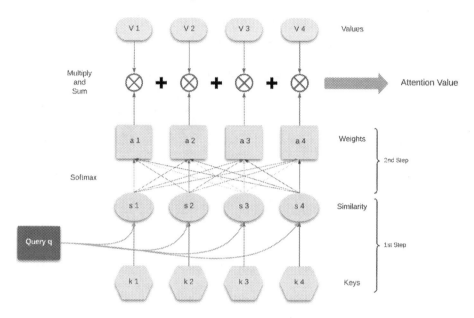

Figure 3-3. *The attention mechanism workflow*

These components work together to compute attention scores that determine how much each element contributes to the representation of the current element. The context vector obtained through the weighted sum of Value vectors reflects the importance of different elements in the sequence relative to the current element.

To better understand the attention mechanism workflow, let us look at a simplified code example of how attention scores are calculated. We will use Python for this.

We will need Numpy and Scipy libraries in Python for this.

```
import numpy as np
from numpy import array
from numpy import random
from scipy.special import softmax
```

We will start by defining the embeddings of four words. In practice, these word embeddings are calculated. But for simplicity we will define them manually here.

```
word_1_em = array([1, 1, 0])
word_2_em = array([0, 1, 1])
word_3_em = array([1, 0, 1])
word_4_em = array([0, 0, 1])
```

We will stack these together to get the word matrix.

```
words = np.stack((word_1_em, word_2_em, word_3_em, word_4_em))

print(words)

Output:
[[1 1 0]
 [0 1 1]
 [1 0 1]
 [0 0 1]]
```

Next, we will initialize the weight matrices for queries, keys, and values. The word embeddings will be multiplied with these to generate the query, key, and value matrices in the next step. In practice, these weights will be learned by the model during training. Here we are initializing them with random values for simplicity.

```
W_Q = random.randint(3, size=(3, 3))
W_K = random.randint(3, size=(3, 3))
W_V = random.randint(3, size=(3, 3))
```

Now we can generate the query, key, and value matrices using matrix multiplication.

```
Q = words @ W_Q
K = words @ W_K
V = words @ W_V
```

Note   The @ operator is used for matrix multiplication in Python. It was introduced in Python 3.5.

We then calculate the score values for the queries against all the key vectors, again using matrix multiplication.

```
scores = Q @ K.transpose()
```

The score values are then passed to the softmax function to calculate the weight values. Typically, at this step, the score values are divided by the square root of their dimensionality before being passed to the softmax function. This is done to overcome the vanishing gradient problem. This approach is known as the *scaled dot product*. We will discuss it in detail in the next section.

```
weights = softmax(scores / K.shape[1] ** 0.5, axis=1)
```

Finally, the attention values for the words can be calculated using these weights.

```
attention = weights @ V

print(attention)
```

Output:
```
[[3.11697171 1.70806649 1.86853077]
 [2.97681807 1.62234515 1.91717725]
 [2.98420993 1.74276532 1.94358637]
 [2.59605139 1.68473833 2.12315889]]
```

The complete code for this example looks like this:

```
import numpy as np
from numpy import array
from numpy import random
from scipy.special import softmax
```

```
# setting the seed for the random functions, allowing us to
reproduce the values
random.seed(101)

# defining word embeddings of 4 words
word_1_em = array([1, 1, 0])
word_2_em = array([0, 1, 1])
word_3_em = array([1, 0, 1])
word_4_em = array([0, 0, 1])

# stacking all the words to get a single word matrix
words = np.stack((word_1_em, word_2_em, word_3_em, word_4_em))

print(words)

# randomly initialize the weight matrices for queries, keys,
and values
W_Q = random.randint(3, size=(3, 3))
W_K = random.randint(3, size=(3, 3))
W_V = random.randint(3, size=(3, 3))

# generating the query, key, and value matrices
Q = words @ W_Q
K = words @ W_K
V = words @ W_V

# calculating the scores for the queries against all
key vectors
scores = Q @ K.transpose()

# computing the weights using softmax operation
weights = softmax(scores / K.shape[1] ** 0.5, axis=1)

# computing the attention by a weighted sum of the
value vectors
```

```
attention = weights @ V

print(attention)
```

The attention mechanism enables the model to capture relationships and dependencies between elements and is a fundamental building block in sequence modeling tasks.

The Transformer Architecture

The paper "Attention Is All You Need" explains that while recurrent neural network (RNN) architectures such as long short-term memory (LSTM) and gated recurrent networks (GRN) have firmly established at the time as the de facto approaches for sequence modeling tasks such as language modeling and machine translation, progress to push their capabilities further has been slow due to some fundamental limitations of such architectures. RNN-based models have limited parallelization options because they naturally require sequential computing.

The transformer architecture overcomes this limitation by forgoing any recurrent components and instead relying entirely on attention mechanisms. ConvS2S and ByteNet models, which were used for sequence-to-sequence modeling prior to transformers, require an increasing number of operations to calculate long-range dependencies as the distance between the elements increases. The number of operations in ConvS2S increases linearly and logarithmically in ByteNet with the distance. In transformers, with self-attention, this can be reduced to a constant number of operations.

Self-attention, also known as *intra-attention*, is a generalized version of traditional attention mechanisms that relate different positions of a single sequence to build a representation of the sequence. By using self-attention, the transformers architecture is able to both parallelize the operations as well as improve the performance of single operations.

Figure 3-4 shows the architecture of a transformer.

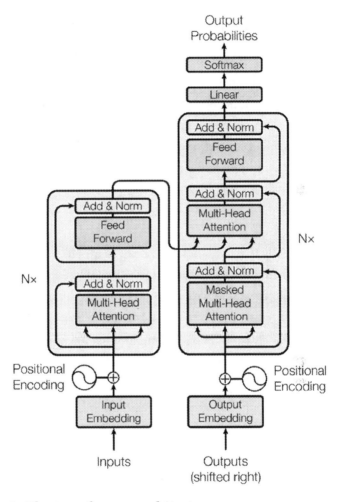

Figure 3-4. *The transformer architecture*

The following are the components of the transformer architecture:

- Tokenizers, which convert text into tokens

- Embedding layers, which convert tokens into semantically meaningful representations

- Transformer layers, which carry out the reasoning capabilities, and consist of attention and multilayer perceptron (MLP) layers

The transformer layers can be of two types: encoder and decoder.

The original architecture of Vaswani et al. used both encoders and decoders. Some later variations of the transformer model used one or the other, such as generative pre-trained transformer(GPT) models, which are decoder-only, while bidirectional encoder representations from Transformers (BERT) models are encoder-only.

The Encoder

Transformers typically use byte pair encoding to tokenize the input. Unlike many other NLP architectures that use traditional word embeddings like Word2Vec or GloVe, transformer models are unique in using a combination of token embeddings, positional encodings, and other specialized embeddings (such as segment embeddings in BERT) to effectively capture both content and sequential context. In more recent variants of transformers (such as GPT-3 and beyond), the concept of subword embeddings and byte pair embeddings has gained prominence. These embeddings enable the model to handle out-of-vocabulary words and provide a more fine-grained representation of words by breaking them down into smaller units.

The encoder, shown in Figure 3-5, is a stack of N identical layers. In the implementation of the original paper, this was set to 6 layers (N=6). Each of these layers is composed of two sublayers, which are as follows:

- The first is a multihead self-attention mechanism.

- The second is a fully connected feed-forward network (multilayer perceptron) consisting of two linear transformations with rectified linear unit (ReLU) activation in between.

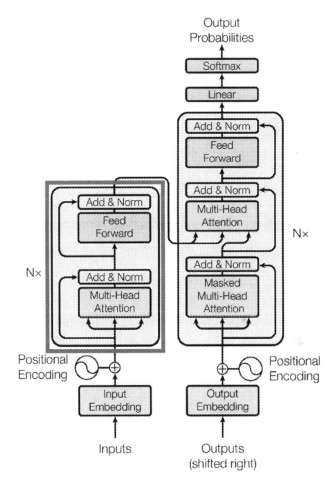

Figure 3-5. *The encoder*

The N layers of a transformer encoder apply the same linear transformations—with each layer employing different weight and bias parameters—to all the words in the input sequence. Each of the two sublayers has a residual connection around them and is succeeded by a normalization layer.

The encoder's main goal is to capture relevant information from the input sequence and create a higher-level representation that can be used by downstream tasks or passed to the decoder for generating output sequences.

As the transformer architecture does not use recurrence, it inherently cannot capture information about the relative positions of the words in the sequence. To overcome this, the positional information has to be injected into the input embeddings, which is done by introducing positional encodings.

The positional encoding vectors have the same dimension as the input embeddings. These are generated using sine and cosine functions of different frequencies. Then, they are summed to the input embeddings in order to inject the positional information.

The Decoder

The decoder, shown in Figure 3-6, is a stack of N identical layers. In the implementation of the original paper, this was set to 6 layers (N=6). Each of these layers is composed of three sublayers, which are as follows:

1. The first sublayer receives the output of the previous decoder stack. It then augments it with positional information and implements multihead self-attention over it. The decoder is designed to attend only to the preceding words, as opposed to the encoder, which is designed to attend to all words in the input sequence, disregarding their position in the sequence. Thus, the prediction for a word at a given position will only depend on the known outputs for the words that come before it in the

sequence. This is achieved by introducing a mask over the values that are produced by the scaled multiplication of the Q and K matrices (Query and Key metrics we discussed in attention mechanisms) in the multihead attention mechanism of the decoder.

2. The second sublayer implements a multihead self-attention mechanism similar to the one in the encoder. This multihead mechanism of the decoder receives the queries from the previous decoder sublayer with the keys and values from the output of the encoder, which allows the decoder to attend to all the words in the input sequence.

3. The third sublayer implements a fully connected feed-forward neural network, which is similar to the one in the encoder.

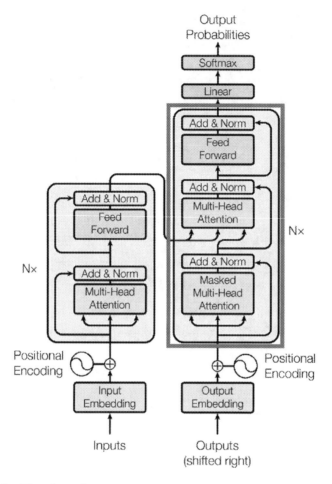

Figure 3-6. *The decoder*

Similar to the encoder, the sublayers on the decoder also have residual connections around them. These sublayers are succeeded by a normalization layer similar to the encoder, and positional encodings are added to the input embeddings in the same way as the encoder.

The output embeddings of the decoder are offset by one position. This, combined with the masking (in the masked multihead attention layer), ensures that the predictions for any given position "will depend only on the known outputs at positions less than i."

Along with the transformer architecture, the original paper introduced two other important concepts: the scaled dot product and multihead attention.

Scaled Dot Product

The scaled dot product was introduced to overcome the vanishing gradient problem. As discussed in the previous chapter, the vanishing gradient problem occurs when the gradient in backpropagation becomes so small that it prevents the network from learning further.

Let us look at a simple code example to understand the scaled dot product.

Note   We are using Python code for the example.

Suppose we create a normal distribution that has a mean of 0 and a standard deviation of 100.

```
a = np.random.normal(0,100,size=(10000))
```

If we plot the histogram of that distribution, it will look like Figure 3-7.

```
plt.hist(a)
```

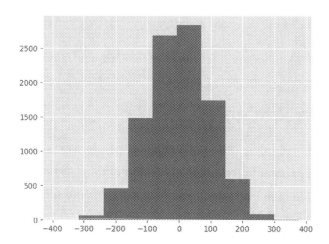

Figure 3-7. *Histogram of a normal distribution that has a mean of 0 and a standard deviation of 100*

If we plot the softmax of the distribution, it will look like Figure 3-8.

```
plt.plot(softmax(a))
```

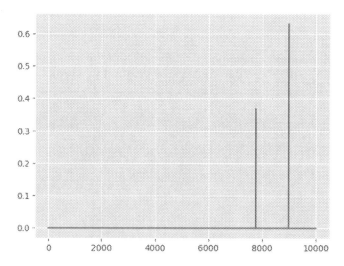

Figure 3-8. *Softmax output of the distribution*

Now, assume we use these softmax values for backpropagation. While the peak values would backpropagate, the other values (which are near zero) would get lost due to their significantly smaller values, resulting in a vanishing gradient.

To overcome this, we can scale the original distribution to a standard deviation of 1 (the original has a standard deviation of 100) by dividing it by the square root of the dimentionality.

```
unit_a = a / 100
```

Plotting the histogram of the original and scaled distributions will look like Figure 3-9.

```
fig, (ax1, ax2) = plt.subplots(1, 2)
ax1.hist(a)
ax2.hist(unit_a)
```

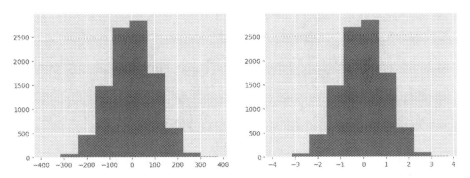

Figure 3-9. *The normal and scaled distributions*

The histograms are identical except for the scale.

If we now plot the softmax of the two distributions, it would look like Figure 3-10.

```
fig, axs = plt.subplots(2, 2)
axs[0, 0].hist(a)
axs[0, 0].set_title('Original Distribution')
```

```
axs[0, 1].hist(unit_a)
axs[0, 1].set_title('Scaled Distribution')
axs[1, 0].plot(softmax(a))
axs[1, 0].set_title('Softmax of Original')
axs[1, 1].plot(softmax(unit_a))
axs[1, 1].set_title('Softmax of Scaled')
```

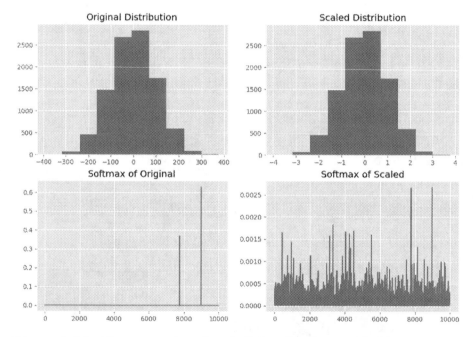

Figure 3-10. *The normal and scaled distributions with their softmax output*

These scaled softmax values have a higher chance of backpropagating properly and allowing the model to train successfully.

The complete code for the previous example is as follows:

```
import numpy as np
import matplotlib.pyplot as plt
from scipy.special import softmax
```

```
from matplotlib import style

plt.style.use('ggplot')

a = np.random.normal(0,100,size=(10000))

plt.hist(a)

plt.plot(softmax(a))

unit_a = a / 100

print(np.std(a))

print(np.std(unit_a))

plt.rcParams['figure.figsize'] = [12, 4]
fig, (ax1, ax2) = plt.subplots(1, 2)
ax1.hist(a)
ax2.hist(unit_a)

plt.rcParams['figure.figsize'] = [12, 8]
fig, axs = plt.subplots(2, 2)
axs[0, 0].hist(a)
axs[0, 0].set_title('Original Distribution')
axs[0, 1].hist(unit_a)
axs[0, 1].set_title('Scaled Distribution')
axs[1, 0].plot(softmax(a))
axs[1, 0].set_title('Softmax of Original')
axs[1, 1].plot(softmax(unit_a))
axs[1, 1].set_title('Softmax of Scaled')
```

In traditional attention modules, there are dot product and softmax operations, making them susceptible to the vanishing gradient problem. As shown, scaling the output of the dot product to have a standard deviation of 1 makes the softmax output less susceptible to the vanishing gradient problem. Figure 3-11 shows the steps of the scaled dot product.

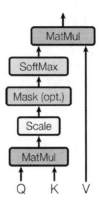

Figure 3-11. *Scaled dot product*

The input of scaled dot product consists of queries and keys (with dimension dk) and values (with dimension dv). The dot products will be computed of the query with all keys, divided each by dk, and finally applying a softmax function to obtain the weights on the values.

Multihead Attention

Instead of using a single attention mechanism multihead attention mechanism linearly projects the queries, keys, and values h times and uses a different learned projection for each of them. Single attention is then applied to each of these h projections in parallel to produce h outputs. These outputs are then concatenated and projected again to produce a final result. Figure 3-12 shows the multihead attention mechanism.

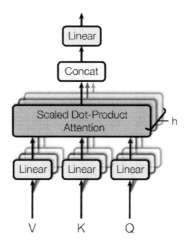

Figure 3-12. *The multihead attention mechanism*

The multihead attention mechanism allows the model to attend to
information from different representation subspaces at different positions,
which is not achievable from a single-head implementation. Figure 3-13
shows an example visualization of how two heads of the same layer have
learned different representations.

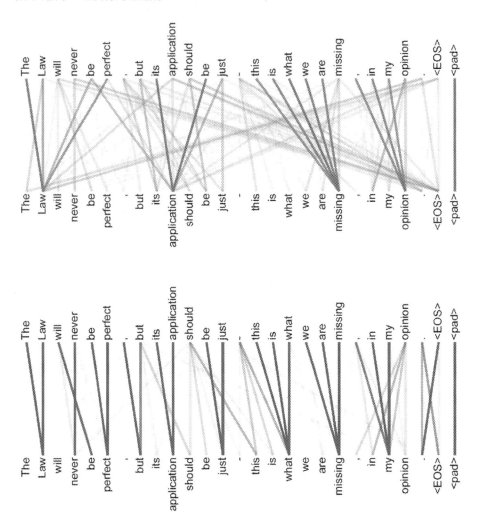

Figure 3-13. *Example visualization of how two heads of the same layer have learned different representations. Source: "Attention Is All You Need" by Vaswani et al.*

With multihead attention, the total computational cost is closer to a single-head attention with full dimensionality because of the reduced dimensionality of each head. This improves the training efficiency massively by allowing parallelism as well as improved efficiency in each parallel path.

Summary

With our understanding of the core concepts of NLP from the previous chapter, we looked at the transformer architecture and attention mechanism in this chapter. The attention mechanisms allowed language models to focus on the important parts of the input sequence. The transformer architecture took that concept further by focusing entirely on attention mechanisms to overcome the limitations of RNN-based models.

The introduction of the transformer architecture revolutionized the NLP field. The efficiency improvements introduced by it are directly responsible for the emergence of large language models.

Large language models are the topic of our next chapter.

CHAPTER 4

What Makes LLMs Large?

By now you should have a high-level understanding of the concepts of natural language processing and how the transformer architecture and attention mechanisms revolutionized the NLP field and how it changed the way we look at language modeling. Now we are ready to step into our main topic: large language models.

You might be wondering what makes a large language model. Is an LLM the same as a transformer? And, more importantly, why do we call them "large" language models?

Let's find out.

What Makes a Transformer Model an LLM

You may see that in many instances of talking about LLMs that the terms *transformer model* and *large language model* are used interchangeably. However, there is a difference as well as a connection between transformers and LLMs.

A *transformer*, as we learned in the previous chapter, specifically refers to a type of neural network architecture that was introduced in the Google Brain and Google Research paper "Attention Is All You Need" by Vaswani et al. in 2017 (https://arxiv.org/abs/1706.03762). This

© Thimira Amaratunga 2023
T. Amaratunga, *Understanding Large Language Models*,
https://doi.org/10.1007/979-8-8688-0017-7_4

is the architecture that uses the attention mechanism and different arrangements of encoder/decoder blocks for language modeling. There are variations of the model with encoder-decoder, encoder-only, or decoder-only in different implementations catering to different requirements. The capabilities as well as the efficiency of the transformer architecture has made it the basis for many large language models.

The term *large language model* generally refers to a language model that has a large number of parameters and is trained on a massive dataset. As mentioned, most large language models use some variation of the transformer architecture. In terms of AI models, parameters are the aspects of the model that are learned from the training data during the training process. Typically, the larger the number of parameters, the more the model can learn. Modern large language models can have hundreds of billions of parameters. As an example, GPT-3 is estimated to have 175 billion parameters.

Therefore, following factors are what makes a transformer into a large language model.

Number of Parameters

One of the defining features of a "large" language model is the number of parameters it has. More parameters generally mean the model can learn more complex representations of the data, though it also increases computational requirements.

Scale of Data

These models are trained on enormous datasets that can range from hundreds of gigabytes to terabytes in size. This allows them to learn from a wide variety of textual contexts.

Computational Power

Training large language models requires significant computational resources, often involving specialized hardware like GPUs or TPUs running in parallel across multiple machines.

Fine-Tuning and Task Adaptation

Once a large language model is trained, it can be fine-tuned on specific tasks or datasets to improve its performance in specialized applications.

Capabilities

Because of their size and complexity, large language models often display capabilities that surpass smaller models, such as better context understanding, error correction, and even some level of commonsense reasoning.

In summary, a transformer becomes a "large language model" when it is scaled up in terms of parameters, trained on a large and diverse dataset, and optimized to perform a wide array of language tasks effectively.

It should also be noted that transformers are not the only architecture that is capable of building large language models. Recurrent neural network (RNN) models such as long short-term memory (LSTM) networks as well as convolutional neural network (CNN) models are capable of creating large language models. However, because of the groundbreaking performance as well as the training efficiency demonstrated by transformer models, the vast majority of LLMs we see today are based on the transformer architecture.

Why Parameters Matter

The number of parameters in a neural network model is a critical aspect that often corresponds to the model's capacity to learn and represent information. In the context of transformers, the number of parameters represents the following:

- *Capacity to learn*: The number of parameters in a model often relates to its ability to fit a given dataset. With more parameters, a model has a greater capacity to capture nuances and complexities in the data.

- *Expressiveness*: A large number of parameters allows the model to represent more intricate functions, making it possible for the model to generalize better to unseen data, provided it is trained appropriately and doesn't overfit.

- *Memory*: In the context of transformers, having more parameters essentially means that the model has a broader "knowledge" base. For instance, models like GPT-3 with 175 billion parameters have shown an ability to remember and generate information across a vast range of topics.

However, when scaling up a transformer model, there are some trade-offs that need to be considered.

Computational Requirements

As the number of parameters increases, so do the computational requirements for training. Training large models necessitates powerful GPUs or TPUs and can be time-consuming and expensive.

Risk of Overfitting

A model with an excessive number of parameters, when trained on limited data, can memorize the training data (rather than generalizing from it). This results in overfitting, where the model performs well on the training data but poorly on unseen data.

Model Size

Having more parameters means larger model sizes, which can be a concern for deployment, especially on edge devices or in real-time applications.

The unique architecture of transformers provides several aspects that allow the number of parameters to scale up:

- *Depth and width*: Transformers can have many layers (depth), and each layer can have a large number of neurons or attention heads (width). Both factors contribute to the total parameter count.

- *Embedding layers*: The initial embedding layer, which converts input tokens into vectors, can have a significant number of parameters, especially when the vocabulary size is large.

- *Attention mechanisms*: Self-attention mechanisms, which are central to transformer architectures, involve multiple weight matrices that contribute to the overall parameter count.

While increasing the number of parameters generally improves the model's performance on many tasks, many neural network models have a point of diminishing returns. However, recent trends, especially in the development of models like GPT-3, have shown that continually scaling up can lead to surprising improvements in performance, enabling capabilities such as few-shot (where the model is trained to perform tasks with very little labeled data by leveraging its pre-trained knowledge) or even zero-shot (where the model is trained to generalize to tasks without having any labelled data for that specific task) learning. This may indicate that we have not yet reached the limit of the capabilities of transformer models, and the current limitations could be computational power and data scale.

The Scale of Data

The scale of data used to train a model is a crucial component in determining the model's effectiveness, especially for transformers like those used in large language models, because of the following factors.

Model Generalization

The more data a model is exposed to during training, the better its ability to generalize to unseen examples. This is particularly true for models with a large number of parameters. The vast parameter count offers the potential to learn a lot, but it also brings the risk of overfitting. A massive dataset can mitigate this risk.

Diverse Knowledge

A large-scale dataset provides a wealth of diverse information. For a language model, this means understanding different writing styles, topics, facts, and even languages.

Rare Scenarios

Big datasets can capture less common, edge-case scenarios, which might not be present in smaller datasets. This allows the model to respond to more niche queries or situations.

Large language models typically use a combination of existing text corpus as well as sourcing data from the Internet, encompassing websites, books, articles, and other textual content. The following are some of the commonly used corpus:

- *Common Crawl*: This is a vast web corpus collected by crawling the Internet. It contains petabytes of data from billions of web pages and is one of the most extensive datasets available. Models like GPT-3 have been known to use subsets of Common Crawl.

- *Wikipedia*: Because of its comprehensive coverage of knowledge and structured writing, Wikipedia dumps (in various languages) are frequently used for training language models.

- *BooksCorpus*: This contains more than 11,000 books, totaling about 5 billion words, from diverse genres and subjects.

- *OpenSubtitles*: This is a dataset containing subtitles from movies and TV shows. It's especially useful for training conversational models because of its dialogue-heavy content.

- *WebText*: Used by OpenAI for training GPT-2, it's a collection of web pages amounting to about 40GB of text data.

- *Toronto Book Corpus*: This is similar to BooksCorpus but contains different books, amounting to more than 44 million words.

- *English Gigaword*: This contains a significant amount of newswire text data, making it rich in current events and journalistic language.

- *Stanford Question Answering Dataset (SQuAD)*: While it's primarily designed for question-answering tasks, the dataset, which contains passages from Wikipedia and associated questions, can be beneficial in training models to understand context.

- *Microsoft MAchine Reading COmprehension Dataset (MS MARCO)*: This contains real-world questions and answers, making it valuable for training models on practical, user-generated queries.

- *Common datasets for translation tasks*: These include Workshop on Machine Translation (WMT) datasets, European Parliament Proceedings (Europarl), and United Nations documents (MultiUN) for training multilingual models.

- *LM1B*: This is a benchmark dataset for language modeling containing 1 billion words from the One Billion Word Benchmark.

- *Penn Treebank*: While smaller than many other datasets, this is a staple in linguistic and syntactic analyses, containing tagged, parsed, and raw *Wall Street Journal* data.

Gathering the data from these and other corpora, as well as from Internet sources, is followed by a data filtering and cleaning step. This is because not all collected data might be useful. It might have errors, be redundant, or be unsuitable for training. Proper preprocessing, cleaning, and filtering are essential to ensure the model learns from high-quality data. Model-specific per-processing steps such as tokenization are applied afterward.

However, as with the parameters, scaling up the data brings its own challenges.

Computational Overheads

Training on a massive dataset requires high computational power and memory. Parallel processing, often spanning multiple GPUs or TPUs, becomes a necessity.

Storage

Simply storing huge datasets necessitates significant storage solutions, often distributed across multiple devices or cloud storage solutions.

Data Bias

Large datasets sourced from the Internet can contain biases present in the content. This means models can inadvertently learn and perpetuate these biases.

Noise

With scale comes noise. Some incorrect or misleading information may be present in vast datasets, which the model might learn if not properly cleaned.

Transformers, with their attention mechanisms, are particularly suited to benefit from large-scale data. The self-attention mechanism can learn intricate patterns, relationships, and dependencies present in vast datasets, enabling the model to capture deep semantic relationships in language. The breakthroughs observed in models like GPT-2 and GPT-3 can be attributed in part to the enormous scale of data they were trained on. When combined with the models' large parameter counts, this data scale allows them to exhibit remarkable language understanding and generation capabilities.

Types of LLMs

Large language models can be categorized based on various factors such as architecture, training objectives, data types, and applications. Let us see a few of these factors and categorizations.

Based on the Architecture

As we discussed earlier, there are several architectures that can be used to build LLMs.

Transformers

Most of today's large language models, such as Generative Pre-trained Transformer (GPT), Bidirectional Encoder Representations from Transformers (BERT), and Pathways Language Model (PaLM), are based on the Transformer architecture.

Recurrent Neural Networks

Older language models often used recurrent neural networks (RNNs) or variations like long short-term memory (LSTM) and gated recurrent units (GRUs), although these are less common for very large models because of scaling limitations.

Convolutional Neural Networks

Although less common for language tasks, some models have employed CNN architectures for text classification and other NLP tasks.

Based on the Training Objective

The training objectives of large language models can vary based on the specific tasks they are designed to perform or the kinds of abilities they are expected to possess. A single model may have one or more training objectives.

- *Autoregressive models*: Like GPT, these models generate one word at a time and use previously generated words as context for future words.

- *Autoencoding models*: BERT is an example that is trained to predict masked-out words in a sentence, and it processes the entire sequence at once.

- *Sequence-to-sequence (Seq2Seq) models*: These are often used for translation, summarization, and other tasks where both input and output can be of variable lengths. Examples include OpenNMT and Tensor2Tensor (T2T).

- *Hybrid models*: Some models, like XLNet, combine elements of both autoregressive and autoencoding approaches.

Let us look into few of these categories in detail.

Autoregressive Models

Autoregressive models are models trained to generate text one token (usually a word or a subword) at a time. They leverage the concept of *autoregression*, where the prediction of each new token is conditioned on the previously generated tokens.

The following are some key features of autoregressive models.

Sequential Generation

Autoregressive models generate text in a left-to-right manner, predicting one token at a time based on the tokens that have come before it. This is in contrast to "autoencoder" models like BERT, which predict missing words in an entire sequence in parallel.

Contextual Understanding

Because they rely on previously generated text, autoregressive models are good at maintaining context in a conversation or text. This makes them suitable for tasks such as dialogue generation, storytelling, and even code writing.

Long-Range Dependencies

The architecture of these models, especially transformer-based ones like GPT, is capable of handling long-range dependencies in the text, allowing them to generate more coherent and contextually relevant text over extended sequences.

Causal Relationship

Autoregressive models maintain a causal relationship in the sequence where each token is generated based on a fixed history of preceding tokens and not future tokens. This is a crucial feature for many natural language understanding and generation tasks.

The training process of an autoregressive model typically follows these steps:

- *Data preprocessing*: The model is usually trained on large datasets that are tokenized into smaller pieces, like words or subwords.

- *Masking and loss function*: During training, the model uses a mask to ensure that the prediction for a particular token does not have access to future tokens in the sequence. The most common loss function used is the cross-entropy loss between the predicted probabilities and the actual tokens.

- *Parameter optimization*: The model's millions or billions of parameters are adjusted through backpropagation and optimization algorithms like Adam to minimize the loss function.

- *Fine-tuning*: Autoregressive models are often fine-tuned on specific tasks or datasets to make them more effective for specialized applications.

Autoregressive LLMs have many applications, such as the following:

- *Natural language generation*: This includes everything from chatbots to creative writing.

- *Machine translation*: Some autoregressive models are fine-tuned for translating between languages.

- *Summarization*: You can generate concise summaries of long documents.

- *Question answering*: You can generate answers to questions based on context or a given passage.

- *Code generation*: Some specialized autoregressive models can write or complete code based on a prompt.

- *Other NLP tasks*: Though not strictly generative tasks, models like these can be adapted for classification, sentiment analysis, and more by adding specialized layers or training setups.

However, autoregressive models do have some limitations, a few of which are as follows:

- *Speed*: Since autoregressive models generate text one token at a time, they can be slower for generation tasks compared to parallel models.

- *Repetition*: These models can sometimes get stuck in loops and generate repetitive text.

- *Lack of revision*: Once a token is generated, it can't be changed, which may lead to errors accumulating in long sequences.

- *Context limit*: There's a maximum sequence length beyond which the model can't maintain context, due to architectural limitations.

Autoencoding Models

Autoencoding language models are designed to generate a fixed-size representation or "encoding" for a given input text. Unlike autoregressive models, which predict one word at a time based on previous words, autoencoding models take an entire sequence of words as input and predict some of those words in parallel.

The following are some key features of autoencoding models.

Bidirectional Context

These models consider both the preceding and following words to predict a target word, thereby offering a bidirectional context. This is different from autoregressive models, which use only preceding words.

Masked Language Modeling

In training, some words in the input sequence are randomly masked out, and the model tries to predict them.

Fixed-Size Encoding

These models produce a fixed-size vector representation of the entire input sequence. This vector can capture the semantic meaning of the input and can be used for various downstream tasks.

Parallelism

Because masked words are predicted in parallel, training and inference with autoencoding models can be faster for certain types of tasks compared to autoregressive models.

The training of an autoencoding model typically involves the following:

- *Data preprocessing*: Text is tokenized into subwords or words, and some tokens are randomly replaced with a [MASK] token or other special tokens.

- *Objective function*: The model is usually trained using a cross-entropy loss function, where it tries to minimize the difference between the predicted probabilities for the masked words and the actual words.

- *Backpropagation*: Gradients are computed based on the loss, and the model's parameters are updated using optimization algorithms like Adam.

- *Fine-tuning*: Similar to autoregressive models, autoencoding models can be fine-tuned on specific tasks to adapt their capabilities.

The applications of autoencoding LLMs include the following:

- *Text classification*: The fixed-size encoding can be used to classify text into various categories.

- *Named entity recognition*: This can identify entities such as names, places, and organizations in text.

- *Question answering*: This can be adapted to provide specific answers based on the question and a given context.

- *Sentiment analysis*: This can classify the sentiment of a sentence or document as positive, negative, or neutral.

- *Search engines*: This can be used to understand and rank documents relevant to a query.

- *Summarization*: While not as straightforward as using sequence-to-sequence models, BERT-like models can still be adapted for text summarization tasks.

Autoencoding models also have certain limitations.

- *Token limit*: Like autoregressive models, these models also have a maximum sequence length, beyond which they can't process text.

- *Lack of coherency*: For sequence generation tasks, autoencoding models don't naturally generate coherent and contextually relevant sequences as effectively as autoregressive models.

- *Complexity*: These models can be computationally expensive to train, particularly because the bidirectional context requires more computational resources to capture.

- *Ambiguity*: Sometimes the masked word can have multiple plausible replacements, making the task inherently ambiguous. The model is trained to predict the most likely word, which may not always be the most contextually appropriate one.

Sequence-to-Sequence Models

Sequence-to-sequence (Seq2Seq) models are designed to transform an input sequence into an output sequence, where both the input and output sequences can have variable lengths. These models are often employed in tasks like machine translation, text summarization, and speech recognition.

The following are the key features of Seq2Seq models.

Encoder-Decoder Architecture

A typical Seq2Seq model consists of two main components: an encoder that processes the input sequence and compresses the information into a fixed-size "context vector," and a decoder that generates the output sequence based on this context vector.

Attention Mechanisms

Modern Seq2Seq models often use attention mechanisms to allow the decoder to focus on different parts of the input sequence for each element of the output sequence. This is particularly useful for handling long sequences and for tasks where the alignment between input and output is complex.

Variable-Length Sequences

Unlike fixed-size autoencoders, Seq2Seq models can handle input and output sequences of different lengths, making them extremely versatile.

Bidirectional Context in Encoder

The encoder often uses bidirectional layers (e.g., bidirectional LSTMs or GRUs) to capture the context from both directions of the input sequence.

The training of a Seq2Seq model includes the following:

- *Data preparation*: In training, pairs of input-output sequences are needed. For example, in machine translation, you would have pairs of sentences in two different languages.

- *Teacher forcing*: During training, the actual output from the training dataset (not the predicted output) is often fed into the decoder in the next time step to guide learning. This technique is known as *teacher forcing*.

- *Loss function*: A common loss function used is the cross-entropy loss between the predicted output sequence and the actual output sequence.

- *Training algorithms*: Optimization algorithms like Adam or RMSprop are often used to adjust the model parameters to minimize the loss.

- *Fine-tuning*: Seq2Seq models can also be fine-tuned for specific domains or tasks to improve performance.

The following are some of the applications of Seq2Seq LLMs:

- *Machine translation*: Translating text from one language to another

- *Text summarization*: Generating a concise summary for a long document

- *Question answering*: Providing a precise answer to a question based on a given context

- *Speech recognition*: Converting spoken language into written text

- *Image captioning*: Generating textual descriptions of images

- *Dialog systems*: Used in chatbots and virtual assistants for generating conversational responses

The limitations of Seq2Seq models include the following:

- *Complexity*: The encoder-decoder architecture and attention mechanisms make these models computationally intensive to train.

- *Data requirements*: Seq2Seq models often require large annotated datasets, especially for complex tasks like machine translation.

- *Long sequences*: While attention mechanisms have alleviated this issue to some extent, handling extremely long sequences is still challenging due to computational limitations.

- *Lack of interpretability*: The attention mechanism provides some insight, but the models are largely black boxes, making it hard to understand why they make specific decisions.

Hybrid Models

Hybrid language models attempt to combine the strengths of different types of models or incorporate additional features to improve performance in specific tasks. While pure autoregressive, autoencoding, or sequence-to-sequence models are powerful in their own right, each has its limitations. Hybrid models aim to address these by fusing different architectures or techniques.

The following are some common types of hybrid models.

Autoregressive + Autoencoding

One common approach is to combine autoregressive and autoencoding models. For example, you could use an autoencoding model like BERT to generate a fixed-size representation of the input and then feed this into an autoregressive model like GPT to generate output text. This could be useful for tasks where you need both a deep understanding of the input and a coherent output, such as in complex question-answering systems.

Seq2Seq + Attention

While attention mechanisms are commonly used in Seq2Seq models, advanced hybrid versions might incorporate multiple types of attention mechanisms or mix attention with other techniques such as reinforcement learning for better performance.

Incorporating External Knowledge

Some hybrid models are designed to interface with external databases or knowledge graphs, allowing them to pull in real-world facts when generating text.

Multimodal Models

These are hybrid models designed to handle multiple types of input (e.g., text and images or text and audio). GPT-3, for instance, has been adapted to generate image captions based on both text prompts and the images themselves.

Classifier + Generator

In tasks such as sentiment analysis followed by text generation, a classification model may first determine the sentiment of the input, and then an autoregressive model could generate a response that aligns with that sentiment.

Because of their nature, some unique training techniques are used with hybrid models, such as the following:

- *Multi-objective loss function*: When you're combining different model types, you often have to optimize a loss function that's a combination of the loss functions appropriate for each individual model.

- *Two-step training*: Sometimes, one part of the model is trained first, followed by the second part. For example, an autoencoder could be pre-trained on a large dataset and then fine-tuned along with an autoregressive model on a specific task.

- *End-to-end training*: In some cases, the entire hybrid model is trained together from scratch, although this can be computationally expensive.

Some of the unique use cases of hybrid models include the following:

- *Advanced question-answering*: Hybrid models can be particularly effective for generating accurate and contextually relevant answers to complex questions.

- *Summarization*: Combining the strengths of different model types could lead to more coherent and factually accurate summaries.

- *Multimodal tasks*: When tasks involve multiple types of data, like text and images, hybrid models can be particularly effective.

Although they have their benefits, hybrid models have their own set of limitations.

- *Computational complexity*: Combining different architectures can lead to models that are even more computationally intensive to train and deploy.

- *Overfitting*: With more parameters and complexity, there's an increased risk of overfitting, especially when not enough data is available.

- *Interpretability*: As models get more complex, it becomes increasingly difficult to understand why they make certain decisions.

- *Engineering challenges*: Building and maintaining hybrid models can be more complex and require specialized expertise.

Because the term *hybrid* is quite broad, it can be applied to a variety of architectures and is not limited to the previous examples. The overarching theme is the attempt to combine different techniques or models to overcome the limitations of using any single approach.

Other Training Objectives

Other than the language modeling objectives we discussed earlier, LLMs may have other training objectives associated with them based on their intended use. Some of these are as follows:

Text Classification Objectives

- *Sentiment analysis*: The objective is to classify the sentiment expressed in a text as positive, negative, or neutral.

- Topic *classification*: The model is trained to categorize texts into predefined topics or classes.

Information Retrieval Objectives

- *Document ranking*: The objective is to rank a set of documents based on their relevance to a query.

- *Keyword extraction*: The objective is to extract important terms or phrases from larger bodies of text.

Multimodal Objectives

- *Image-text association*: In multimodal models like CLIP and DALL-E, the model is trained to understand and generate associations between text and images.

- *Audio-text association*: Some models are trained to transcribe or understand spoken language and its relationship to written text.

Specialized Objectives

- *Named entity recognition (NER)*: The objective is to identify named entities such as people, organizations, locations, etc., in a text.

- *Part-of-speech tagging*: The model is trained to identify the part of speech for each word in a sentence.

- *Dependency parsing*: The objective is to identify grammatical relationships between words.

- *Text generation*: Some models are specialized for creative text generation, including poetry, storytelling, and more.

Other Objectives

- *Few-shot learning*: The model is trained to perform tasks with very little labeled data by leveraging its pre-trained knowledge.

- *Zero-shot learning*: The model is trained to generalize to tasks without having any labeled data for that specific task, often by understanding the task description in natural language.

- *Multitask learning*: The model is trained to perform multiple tasks simultaneously, often sharing a common representation to improve performance across tasks.

- *Adversarial training*: To improve robustness, some models are trained to withstand adversarial attacks, where small, carefully crafted changes to the input can mislead the model.

Different training objectives are often combined to create more versatile models, and task-specific objectives are often tackled by fine-tuning a pre-trained general-purpose model.

Usage-Based Categorizations

Apart from the architecture and the objectives, LLMs can also be broadly categorized based on their usage and input. The following are a few of those categories:

Based on Data Types

- *Text-based models*: Most large language models are trained primarily on text data.

- *Multimodal models*: These models are trained on multiple types of data, like text and images. DALL-E and CLIP by OpenAI are examples.

- *Cross-lingual models*: These are trained on text from multiple languages and can perform tasks across different languages without needing separate training for each.

Based on Applications

- *General-purpose models*: These are designed to handle a variety of tasks without being specialized for any particular one. Examples include GPT and BERT.

- *Task-specific models*: These are fine-tuned versions of general-purpose models, adapted for specific tasks such as text classification, sentiment analysis, or machine translation.

- *Domain-specific models*: These are trained or fine-tuned on specialized data from fields such as healthcare, law, or finance.

- *Conversational agents*: Some large language models, like Meena by Google, are designed to improve conversational abilities for chatbots and virtual assistants.

- *Code generation models*: Models like GitHub's Copilot are specialized for generating code based on natural language queries.

Different types of large language models may overlap in their characteristics. The landscape is continually evolving, with new types and hybrids appearing as the field progresses.

Foundation Models

The term *foundation models* emphasizes the shift in machine learning from training models for individual tasks to a paradigm where a single, powerful model can serve as a foundation for a multitude of applications.

Foundation models refer to pre-trained models, typically of considerable size and capacity, that serve as a base or "foundation" upon which more specific applications or tasks can be built. While the term can technically apply to various domains, it's often used in the context of large-scale machine learning models, especially in natural language processing.

The following are some key characteristics of foundation models.

Pre-training on Broad Data

Foundation models are typically trained on vast and diverse datasets to learn a wide array of patterns, structures, and knowledge. This generalist pre-training phase is what enables them to serve as a "foundation."

Fine-Tuning and Adaptability

Once pre-trained, foundation models can be fine-tuned or adapted to specific tasks or domains, inheriting the general knowledge from pre-training and specializing based on new, task-specific data.

Transfer Learning

The essence of foundation models lies in transfer learning, where knowledge gained during one task is transferred to improve performance on a different, yet related, task.

Economies of Scale

Given the resources required to train large models, it's often more efficient to train a single, large foundation model that can serve multiple purposes rather than training separate models for each specific task.

Large language models are considered foundation models because they exhibit properties and characteristics that position them as foundational building blocks for a plethora of applications.

The following are some of the characteristics of LLMs that make them foundation models.

General-Purpose Abilities

LLMs are trained on vast and diverse text corpora, enabling them to handle a wide range of tasks out of the box, from simple text generation to more complex tasks such as summarization, translation, and question-answering.

Fine-Tuning Capabilities

Once pre-trained on a broad dataset, LLMs can be fine-tuned on specific tasks or domain-specific data, making them adaptable to various specialized applications.

Transfer Learning

The knowledge captured by LLMs during their extensive pre-training can be transferred and utilized in numerous applications, reducing the need for task-specific data or training.

Economies of Scale

Training LLMs requires significant computational resources. But once trained, they can serve countless applications, providing a cost-benefit when distributed across multiple tasks or domains.

Rapid Deployment

With LLMs as a foundation, developers can rapidly prototype and deploy applications. For instance, with just a well-crafted prompt, GPT-3 can perform tasks that traditionally would require specialized models.

Interdisciplinary Applications

Beyond text-centric tasks, LLMs have been utilized in areas like code generation, art creation, and even scientific domains, underscoring their foundational nature.

Reduced Training Overhead

Instead of training a model from scratch for every specific task, developers can leverage the foundational knowledge of LLMs, reducing the data requirements and computational overhead for many applications.

Continuous Adaptability

LLMs have the potential to adapt to new information and trends either by continuous training or by combining them with other models and systems.

Democratization of AI

Given the right interfaces and platforms, nonexperts can tap into the capabilities of LLMs, enabling a broader set of users to benefit from AI without deep technical knowledge.

Applying LLMs

While having general-purpose abilities, when applying large language models for a specific task or a domain, often you would need to tune them for that specific task or domain in order for them to be more effective in it. This can be done in two ways: using prompt engineering and/or using fine-tuning.

Prompt Engineering

Prompt engineering refers to the art and science of crafting effective input prompts to guide the behavior of large language models, especially when seeking specific or nuanced responses. As large models like GPT-3 or GPT-4 do not have traditional "task-specific" configurations, the way you phrase or structure the input prompt can significantly influence the output. This has been especially noted in zero-shot, few-shot, or many-shot learning scenarios.

The following are the key aspects of prompt engineering:

- *Precision*: Crafting prompts that help the model understand exactly what kind of information or format you are seeking.

- *Context*: Providing enough background or context to guide the model to generate relevant outputs.

- *Examples*: In few-shot learning scenarios, giving the model a couple of examples to demonstrate the desired task can help in eliciting the right kind of response.

- *Rephrasing*: If a model doesn't produce the desired output with a given prompt, rephrasing the question or request might yield better results.

- *Constraints*: Specifying constraints in the prompt to restrict or guide the model's responses. For instance, asking the model to "explain in simple terms" or "provide an answer in less than 50 words."

In terms of LLMs, the following principles can be used for optimizing the prompts.

Explicitness

Being clear and precise in the instruction can help the model grasp the exact requirement. For instance, instead of asking "Tell me about apples," you might say "Provide a 200-word summary about the nutritional benefits of apples."

110

Examples as Guidance

Providing examples can be a way to demonstrate the expected output. For instance, if you're trying to get the model to transform sentences into questions, you might provide an example: "Transform the following sentences into questions. Example: 'It is raining' becomes 'Is it raining?'"

Iterative Refinement

Prompt engineering often involves an iterative process of refining the input based on the outputs received. If a particular phrasing doesn't work, rephrasing or providing additional context can be helpful.

Controlling Verbosity and Complexity

Directives like "in simple terms," "briefly explain," or "in detail" can guide the length and depth of the model's response.

Systematic Variations

Trying systematic variations of prompts helps in understanding the kind of phrasing that works best for a particular task.

Prompt engineering is extremely important because of the following factors:

- *Optimal outputs*: Even with a highly capable model, the quality of the output often depends on how the input is framed. Effective prompt engineering ensures you're getting the most out of the model.

- *Handling ambiguity*: Language can be inherently ambiguous. By refining prompts, users can reduce ambiguity and guide the model toward the most relevant interpretation of their query.

- *Task customization*: Since large models like GPT-3 aren't trained for specific tasks in the traditional sense, prompt engineering allows users to effectively "customize" the model for a wide array of tasks without needing to retrain it.

There are several techniques that can be employed to engineer prompts when working with LLMs:

- *Prompt templates*: Creating templates where only specific parts of the prompt change can help in achieving consistency, especially in tasks like data extraction.

- *Prompt concatenation*: Sometimes combining multiple prompts or instructions in a sequence can guide the model better. For instance, "Translate the following English text to French. Ensure the translation is suitable for a formal business setting."

- *Question decomposition*: For complex queries, breaking down the prompt into multiple simpler questions might yield more accurate answers.

- *Prompt priming*: Introducing a context or "priming" the model with a statement can sometimes help. For example, "Pretend you are a history teacher. Explain the significance of the Renaissance period."

Prompt engineering gives several benefits when applying LLMs to specific tasks:

- *Versatility*: Through prompt engineering, a single pre-trained model can be "repurposed" for a wide array of tasks without the need for fine-tuning.

- *Efficiency*: It offers a quicker way to adapt the model to new tasks, especially when compared to retraining or fine-tuning.

- *Customizability*: Different users or applications might have unique requirements, and prompt engineering provides a way to customize model outputs without changing the underlying model.

However, there are some limitations and challenges with prompt engineering as well:

- *Inconsistency*: Even with an optimized prompt, models might occasionally produce inconsistent or unexpected outputs.

- *Overhead*: Effective prompt engineering can require extensive trial and error, which might be computationally or time-expensive.

- *Domain limitations*: For very niche or specialized tasks, prompt engineering might not suffice to achieve high accuracy, and fine-tuning on domain-specific data might be necessary.

- *Trial and error*: Finding the right prompt might require several iterations, especially for complex or nuanced tasks.

- *Overfitting to prompts*: If users are too specific or rely heavily on prompt examples, the model might overfit to those examples, which can reduce the generality of its outputs.

- *Predictability*: Even with good prompts, the inherent randomness in model outputs means results might not always be entirely consistent.

Prompt engineering is a blend of understanding the model's capabilities, linguistic nuances, and the specific requirements of a task. As transformer-based models grow in size and capability, prompt engineering stands out as a crucial skill to harness their potential fully. It's an active area of research and experimentation, with both the AI research community and industry professionals exploring novel strategies to optimize interactions with these models.

Fine-Tuning

In certain scenarios, domains, or tasks, prompt engineering alone may not yield the required results. In such cases model fine-tuning may be needed.

Fine-tuning is the process of adapting a pre-trained large language model to a specific task or domain, capitalizing on the general knowledge the model has acquired and tailoring it to be more effective for specialized applications.

LLMs are initially pre-trained on a vast and diverse text corpora. During this phase, the model learns language structures, grammar, facts, reasoning abilities, and even some biases present in the data. This general training yields a model that's knowledgeable but not necessarily specialized in any particular task.

After pre-training, the model can be further trained (or "fine-tuned") on a smaller, narrower, task-specific dataset. This dataset is typically labeled and relates to a specific application, such as sentiment analysis, question answering, or medical text classification.

This provides several benefits:

- *Specialization*: While the pre-trained model is a jack-of-all-trades, fine-tuning tailors it to be an expert in a particular domain or task.

- *Transfer learning*: Fine-tuning leverages the general knowledge gained during pre-training, allowing the model to achieve strong performance on specific tasks even with a smaller amount of task-specific data.

- *Efficiency*: Training a model from scratch on a specific task might require a vast amount of data and computational resources. Fine-tuning a pre-trained model can achieve competitive, if not superior, results with less data and in less time.

For fine-tuning, you need a labeled dataset corresponding to your specific task. For instance, if you're fine-tuning for sentiment analysis, you'd need a dataset of sentences/paragraphs labeled as positive, negative, or neutral.

Instead of initializing the model with random weights (as you would when training from scratch), you start with the weights from the pre-trained model. You then update these weights using your task-specific data.

A crucial aspect of fine-tuning is selecting an appropriate learning rate. Often, a smaller learning rate is chosen compared to pre-training because you want to make smaller adjustments to the already learned weights, rather than significant changes.

However, when attempting to fine-tune an LLM, several key aspects needs to be considered.

Overfitting

Given that LLMs have a massive number of parameters, they can easily overfit to a small fine-tuning dataset. Regularization techniques, early stopping, or even using a smaller version of the pre-trained model can help mitigate this.

Catastrophic Forgetting

If fine-tuned too aggressively, the model might "forget" some of the general knowledge it acquired during pre-training. A balanced approach is necessary to retain the general knowledge while adapting to the specific task.

Evaluation

Always evaluate the fine-tuned model on a separate validation or test set to gauge its performance on the specific task.

Fine-tuning is a powerful mechanism in the transfer learning paradigm that allows developers to harness the might of LLMs for a wide range of tasks without the need for vast amounts of labeled data or extensive training times.

Summary

In this chapter, we discussed what factors make a transformer model into a large language model and how factors such as parameter count and the scale of data affect their capabilities. We talked about how LLMs can be categorized using different perspectives such as their architecture, training objectives, and applications. We looked at the concept of foundation models, and how LLMs possess those characteristics. Finally, we looked at how prompt engineering and fine-tuning can be used to adapt LLMs to specific tasks more effectively.

In the next chapter, we will look at several of the popular LLMs, their architectures, and capabilities.

CHAPTER 5

Popular LLMs

Over the past couple of chapters, we have discussed the history of NLP, its concepts, and how it evolved over time. We learned about the transformer architecture and how it revolutionized how we look at language models and paved the way for LLMs.

Now, with that understanding, we should look at some of the most influential LLMs in recent years.

Although the field has been around for only a couple of years, the number of innovations in the LLM space has been massive. With new and improved models being released frequently and some models being proprietary in nature, it is not easy to talk about every variation. But here, we have made a list of some of the most impactful models and their details that are publicly available.

Generative Pre-trained Transformer

Generative Pre-trained Transformer (GPT) is the model that popularized LLMs to the general public. GPT is a family of LLMs released by OpenAI, an American artificial intelligence research laboratory consisting of the nonprofit OpenAI Inc. and its for-profit subsidiary, OpenAI LP. The GPT models are a collection of foundation models based on the transformer architecture that have been sequentially numbered, referred to as the "GPT-n" series, with GPT-1 being the first and GPT-4 being the most recent.

© Thimira Amaratunga 2023
T. Amaratunga, *Understanding Large Language Models*,
https://doi.org/10.1007/979-8-8688-0017-7_5

In 2018, OpenAI published an article titled "Improving Language Understanding by Generative Pre-Training." In this article, they introduced the first GPT system, which later became known as GPT-1. The introduction of the transformer model in 2017 marked the beginning of pre-trained transformer models, which are generative.

As we learned in the earlier chapters, prior to the introduction of the transformer model, neural NLP models primarily employed supervised learning from large amounts of manually labeled data. This reliance on supervised learning limited their use of datasets that were not well-annotated. In addition, the limited parallelization of those models made training extremely large models prohibitively expensive and time-consuming. Therefore, some languages, such as Swahili or Haitian Creole, were deemed near impossible to model using those methods because of a lack of available text for corpus-building.

To overcome these limitations, OpenAI's GPT model used a semi-supervised approach, which was the first time such an approach was used with transformer models. The approach involved two stages:

1. An unsupervised generative pre-training stage in which a language modeling objective was used to set initial parameters

2. A supervised discriminative "fine-tuning" stage in which these parameters were adapted to a target task

The first GPT architecture (GPT-1) used a 12-layer decoder-only transformer, using 12 masked self-attention heads, with 64-dimensional states each (for a total of 768), followed by linear-softmax. For the position-wise feed-forward networks, 3,072-dimensional inner states were used. Figure 5-1 shows the architecture of GPT-1.

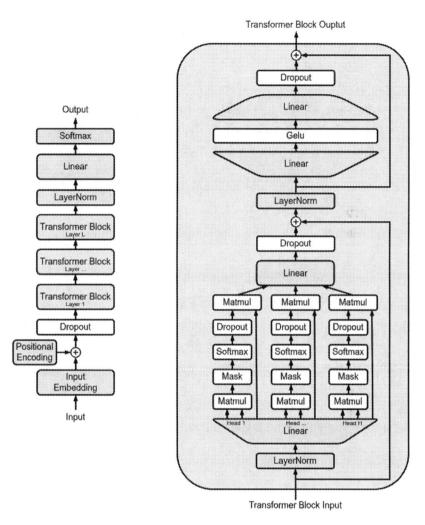

Figure 5-1. *The architecture of GPT-1. Source: "Improving Language Understanding by Generative Pre-Training," OpenAI*

The model used the Adam optimization algorithm rather than the more commonly used stochastic gradient descent (SGD). The learning rate was increased linearly from zero over the first 2,000 updates to a maximum of 2.5×10^{-4}, and annealed to 0 using a cosine schedule. The model used mini-batches of 64 randomly sampled, contiguous sequences of 512 tokens and was trained for 100 epochs. The model used bytepair encoding vocabulary with 40,000 merges and residual, embedding, and attention dropouts with a rate of 0.1 for regularization, also employing a modified version of L2 regularization with w = 0.01 on all nonbias or gain weights. Gaussian Error Linear Unit (GELU) was used as the activation function.

Hyperparameter settings from the unsupervised pre-training stage were reused for the most part in the fine-tuning stage. A 0.1 dropout rate has been added to the classifier, and a learning rate of 6.25e-5 and a batchsize of 32 has been used. The model used a linear learning rate decay schedule with warmup over 0.2 percent of training and a λ value of 0.5. OpenAI has noted that GPT-1 can sufficiently adapt to most tasks with just three epochs of fine-tuning.

GPT-1 was trained on BookCorpus, a dataset consisting of the text of around 11,000 unpublished books scraped from the Internet. BookCorpus (also known as the Toronto Book Corpus) was introduced in a 2015 paper by researchers from the University of Toronto and MIT titled "Aligning Books and Movies: Towards Story-like Visual Explanations by Watching Movies and Reading Books" as a dataset consisting of free books written by yet unpublished authors. The dataset consists of around 985 million words, and the books that comprise it span a range of genres, such as science fiction, romance, and fantasy. GPT-1 used a subset of the BookCorpus dataset, which was around 7,000 books and was chosen to contain the long passages of continuous text that helped the model learn to handle long-range dependencies. The raw text of the dataset was cleaned using the FTFY library (a heuristic-based Python library designed by Robyn Speer at Luminoso that is used for fixing broken Unicode text), followed by standardization of whitespace and punctuation. The tokenization was done using the spaCy library, an open-source library for Python and Cython for part-of-speech tagging, named entity recognition (NER), text categorization, and dependency parsing, which uses convolutional neural network models.

GPT-2, the successor of GPT-1, was partially released in February 2019, which was followed by the release of the full 1.5-billion-parameter model in November 2019. The reason for the controlled release was concerns about potential misuse, including generating fake news or malicious content due to the capabilities displayed by the model. One of GPT-2's main strengths is its ability to generate coherent and contextually relevant text. Given a prompt or partial sentence, GPT-2 can generate complete, realistic, and contextually appropriate text.

For the training of GPT-2, the CommonCrawl corpus was initially considered because of its large size. CommonCrawl is a large text corpus created using web crawling and was commonly used in training NLP systems. However, it was later rejected as a training dataset as data quality issues and unintelligible content were found during the initial reviews of GPT-2 training. Instead, OpenAI created a new corpus, known as WebText, specifically for training GPT models. Unlike CommonCrawl, WebText was generated by scraping only pages linked to Reddit posts, with the condition that the post has received at least three upvotes prior to December 2017, as opposed to scraping content indiscriminately from the web, which was done in previous datasets such as CommonCrawl. The scraped data of WebText was then cleaned, HTML documents were parsed into plain text, duplicate pages were eliminated, and Wikipedia pages were removed from the dataset since their presence in many other datasets could have induced overfitting.

OpenAI first announced GPT-2 in February 2019. However, OpenAI refused to publicly release the GPT -2's source code initially in contrast to GPT-1, which was made available immediately upon announcement. OpenAI cited that the reluctance was due to the risk of malicious use. Initial concerns on GPT-2 were its potential ability to generate text that can be considered obscene or racist or that spammers can use the generated text to exploit and evade automated filters since the generated text was usually completely novel.

Because of these concerns, OpenAI opted not to release the fully trained model for GPT-2 nor detail the corpora it was trained on with the February 2019 announcement. However, researchers were able to replicate GPT-2 using the descriptions of OpenAI's methods in prior publications and the free availability of the underlying code of earlier models. OpenGPT-2 was one such replication. It was released in August 2019. Along with it, a freely licensed version of WebText called OpenWebText was also released. OpenAI released a partial version of GPT-2 in August 2019. This version had 774 million parameters, which was roughly half the size of the full model, which had 1.5 billion parameters.

By November 2019, OpenAI stated that they had not seen strong evidence of misuse so far, and the full 1.5 billion parameter model was released in November 2019.

In May 2020, OpenAI announced GPT-3. While architecturally similar to earlier GPT models, it has higher accuracy. This is attributed to its increased capacity and greater number of parameters. It uses a 2,048-tokens-long context and then-unprecedented size of 175 billion parameters, requiring 800GB to store. The model demonstrated strong zero-shot and few-shot learning on many tasks.

GPT-3 was trained on the following data:

- 60 percent of the data was from a filtered version of Common Crawl consisting of 410 billion byte-pair-encoded tokens

- 22 percent of the data was from WebText2, consisting of 19 billion tokens

- 8 percent of the data was from 12 billion tokens of the Books1 dataset

- 8 percent of the data was from 55 billion tokens from the Books2 dataset

- 2 percent of the data was from 3 billion tokens from Wikipedia

Note   OpenAI has not disclosed the origin or the contents of Books1 or Books2 at the time of this writing.

The capabilities of GPT-3 directly lead to the concept of prompt engineering.

With the success of the GPT-3 model, OpenAI has released a family of GPT-3 models that can be utilized for different purposes.

Model Name	# of Parameters
GPT-3 Small	125 million
GPT-3 Medium – "Ada"	350 million
GPT-3 Large	760 million
GPT-3 XL – "Babbage"	1.3 billion
GPT-3 2.7B	2.7 billion
GPT-3 6.7B – "Curie"	6.7 billion
GPT-3 13B	13 billion
GPT-3 175B – "DaVinci"	175 billion

In March 2022, OpenAI made available new versions of GPT-3 and OpenAI Codex in its API with edit and insert capabilities under the names "text-davinci-002" and "code-davinci-002."

Codex is a variation of the GPT-3 model, fine-tuned for use in programming applications, which gives the ability to parse natural language and generate code in response. In March 2023, concerns raised by the software community caused OpenAI to shut down access to Codex. The main concerns were whether the code snippets generated by Codex could violate copyright (in particular, the GPL condition requiring derivative works to be licensed under equivalent terms) and whether training on public repositories falls into fair use. The Codex model is now available to be used only by researchers of the OpenAI Research Access Program.

In November 2022, OpenAI began referring to the text-davinci and code-davinci models as belonging to the "GPT-3.5" series. At the same time, they released ChatGPT, a GPT-3.5 model fine-tuned for conversations. ChatGPT was notable for allowing users to steer the conversations to generate the desired content by considering the succeeding prompts and replies as context.

In April 2023, OpenAI introduced a new variant of its GPT-3.5 series model, known as "GPT-3.5 with Browsing," building upon the capabilities of its predecessors text-davinci-002 and code-davinci-002, and incorporating the ability to access and browse online information leading to more accurate and up-to-date responses to user queries. The GPT-3.5 with Browsing model was made available to the public in April 2023.

GPT-3 marked the transition of the GPT-n family from open source to proprietary models. In September 2020, Microsoft announced that it had licensed exclusive use of GPT-3. While others can still use the public API to receive output, only Microsoft will have access to GPT-3's underlying model. The architecture details and the training dataset used remain undisclosed.

OpenAI released GPT-4 in March 2023. OpenAI has demonstrated video and image inputs for GPT-4. However, these features remain inaccessible to the general public at this time. OpenAI offers the ChatGPT Plus subscription service, which gives access to a ChatGPT version powered by GPT-4. Microsoft Bing Chat also uses GPT-4. So far, OpenAI has declined to reveal any technical information about GPT-4, such as the size of the model. Experts have, however, speculated that GPT-4 has around 1.8 trillion parameters across 120 layers and has been trained on 13 trillion tokens.

GPT models have had a massive impact on the NLP field by popularizing LLMs and their capabilities and triggering the creation of competitor models, which keep pushing the boundaries of AI.

Bidirectional Encoder Representations from Transformers

Bidirectional Encoder Representations from Transformers (BERT) was introduced in 2018 by researchers at Google Jacob Devlin et al. in their paper titled "BERT: Pre-training of Deep Bidirectional Transformers for Language Understanding." Within a short time, BERT became the baseline for state-of-the-art NLP experimentations, with more than 150 publications citing the model and its improvements.

BERT is an encoder-only transformer model. BERT's innovation lies in its ability to capture context from both forward and backward directions in a sequence, enabling it to create highly contextualized word representations. Unlike earlier traditional language models that were unidirectional (predicting the next word given previous words), BERT predicts missing words in a sentence by considering both the left and right context, allowing it to capture contextual nuances more effectively.

BERT has used the masked language model training objective for its pre-training. During training, random words in sentences are masked, and the model learns to predict these masked words based on the surrounding context. Its bidirectional nature enables it to predict masked words effectively. BERT's input representation involves tokenizing text into subword units (WordPieces) using the WordPiece tokenizer. This technique helps with handling out-of-vocabulary words and breaking down complex words. BERT introduces segment embeddings to distinguish between different sentences in a document or context. These segment embeddings are especially useful for tasks where the model needs an understanding of the relationships between sentences, such as question answering. BERT's output embeddings are contextualized, meaning they capture each word's context concerning the entire sentence. This context awareness contributes to its strong performance in understanding nuances and relationships within the text.

The original English language implementation of the BERT model had two sizes:

- BERT$_{BASE}$: 12 encoders, 12 bidirectional self-attention heads, 110 million parameters in total

- BERT$_{LARGE}$: 4 encoders, 16 bidirectional self-attention heads, 340 million parameters in total

The BASE and LARGE models were pre-trained on the Toronto BookCorpus (800M words) and English Wikipedia (2,500M words).

In October 2019, Google announced that they had started applying BERT models for English language search queries within the United States. In December 2019, it was reported that Google Search had adopted BERT for more than 70 languages. By October 2020, almost every single English-based query was processed by a BERT model.

Pathways Language Model

The Pathways Language Model (PaLM) is a transformer-based large language model developed by Google. The model was first announced in April 2022 and remained private until March 2023. At the time of this writing, the PaLM API was made available for developers through a waitlist, and Google stated that it would be made publicly available later.

The main implementation of PaLM has 540 billion parameters. The researchers have also built two smaller versions of the PaLM model with 8 and 62 billion parameters for different tasks. The PaLM model has demonstrated its capabilities in a wide range of tasks, such as commonsense reasoning, mathematical reasoning, joke explanation, code generation, and language translation. When combined with chain-of-thought prompting (a prompt engineering technique that allows large language models to solve a problem as a series of intermediate steps before giving a final answer), PaLM has achieved significantly better performance on datasets requiring multistep reasoning, such as word problems and logic-based questions.

In January 2023, Google developed an extended version of the PaLM 540B model called Med-PaLM, which was fine-tuned on medical data and outperformed previous models on medical question-answering benchmarks. Med-PaLM became the first AI model to obtain a passing score on U.S. medical licensing questions. It not only was able to answer both multiple-choice and open-ended questions accurately but also provided reasoning and was able to evaluate its own responses.

Google then further extended PaLM using a vision transformer to create PaLM-E, a state-of-the-art vision-language model that can be used for robotic manipulation.

In May 2023, Google announced PaLM 2, which is reported to be a 340 billion parameter model trained on 3.6 trillion tokens.

In June 2023, Google announced AudioPaLM for speech-to-speech translation, which uses the PaLM-2 architecture and initialization.

Large Language Model Meta AI

Large Language Model Meta AI (LLaMA) is a family of large language models developed by Meta AI (an artificial intelligence laboratory belonging to Meta Platforms Inc., formerly known as Facebook, Inc.) starting in February 2023.

The first version of LLaMA had four model sizes trained on 7, 13, 33, and 65 billion parameters, respectively. LLaMA's developers reported that the 13 billion parameter model's performance on most NLP benchmarks exceeded that of the much larger GPT-3, which has 175 billion parameters.

In July 2023, in partnership with Microsoft, Meta announced Llama 2. Llama 2 had three model sizes with 7, 13, and 70 billion parameters, respectively. The model architecture remains largely unchanged from Llama 1 models, but 40 percent more data was used for training.

Compared to GPT-3, LLaMA has these key differences:

- LLaMA uses the SwiGLU activation function instead of ReLU.

- LLaMA uses rotary positional embeddings instead of absolute positional embedding.

- LLaMA uses root-mean-squared layer-normalization instead of standard layer-normalization.

- LLaMA increases context length from 2048 (in Llama 1) tokens to 4096 (in Llama 2) tokens between.

Meta has released the LLaMA's model weights to the research community under a noncommercial license, unlike many other LLMs, which remain proprietary.

Summary

What we discussed in this chapter is only a portion (although some of the most impactful tools) of the LLM landscape. Because some of these models are proprietary, as well as being extremely new, details of their inner workings are scarce. We may get to learn more as time goes on. For the time being, the best way to learn about their capabilities is to experiment with them. AI model repositories such as HuggingFace (`https://huggingface.co`) contains either official or open-source recreations of the models we discussed with instructions to get you started.

As a rapidly developing area, new architectures, improvements, and achievements in the LLM field happens daily. We may yet to see the full capabilities of LLMs.

CHAPTER 6

Threats, Opportunities, and *Misconceptions*

The release of ChatGPT was a significant milestone in AI, not just because of its groundbreaking capabilities and its pushing of the boundaries of technology but also because of the unprecedented interest it generated in the general public. While AI technology components have been part of day-to-day technology for decades, this level of enthusiasm from the general public was previously unheard of.

It was not only the technology enthusiasts or the research community alone. The interest was from people from many other technical and nontechnical fields as well as from media outlets. This popularity, together with the fact that the capabilities of ChatGPT were open to the general public to use, helped it become the fastest-growing consumer software application in history, which in turn directly led to the widespread recognition of large language models (LLMs) and an explosion of competing models from different vendors.

This widespread enthusiasm, as well as the media hype around them, has caused some misunderstandings and misinterpretations of LLMs and their capabilities. This has led to some concern, and in some cases fear, toward LLMs and AI technology in general.

© Thimira Amaratunga 2023
T. Amaratunga, *Understanding Large Language Models*,
https://doi.org/10.1007/979-8-8688-0017-7_6

There are some aspects regarding LLMs that pose legitimate concerns and need to be addressed as the technology progresses and gets applied. However, from the conversations happening about LLMs, it is clear that some of the concerns gaining traction are misplaced.

In this book, we have gone through the history, reasoning, techniques, and various implementations of LLMs. So, with our understanding of how large language models work, let's look into some of the concerns, misconceptions, and opportunities surrounding LLMs.

LLMs and the Threat of a Superintelligent AI

The capabilities of ChatGPT and its counterparts have mesmerized people. Its ability to have human-like conversations and the demonstration of knowledge from a vast set of distinct domains has people considering it to have superhuman abilities. While many have praised these capabilities and are enthusiastic to utilize them, it has brought up a deep-rooted fear: the existential threat from a superintelligent AI.

To understand this better, we must look at the levels of AI.

Levels of AI

The goal of AI research, as we learned in the first chapter, is to build machines that have intelligent behavior. The levels of AI refer to different stages or capabilities of artificial intelligence in that journey. These can depend on everything from simple, rule-based algorithms to hypothetical machines that might one day surpass human intelligence in all areas. These levels are defined to help clarify discussions around AI's capabilities and potential future developments and theoretical capabilities.

The main levels of AI are as follows.

Narrow or weak AI

These are AI systems designed and trained for a specific task. They operate based on a predefined set of rules or models trained on specific data.

Characteristics:

- *Task-specific*: Performs well on one task but lacks versatility

- *No consciousness*: Operates without understanding, emotions, or self-awareness

- *Needs input*: Relies on human-defined parameters

- *Examples*: Image recognition software, chatbots tailored to specific services, and algorithms that recommend videos or songs based on user behavior

Artificial general intelligence (AGI)

AI that has the capability to understand, learn, and perform any intellectual task that a human can, possessing similar cognitive abilities to a human.

Characteristics:

- *Versatility*: Can learn and excel in multiple tasks, not just the ones it was specifically trained for.

- *Learning and adaptation*: Can learn new tasks without being explicitly programmed for them.

- *Conceptual understanding*: Can understand abstract concepts, reason through problems, and make decisions in unfamiliar situations.

- *Examples*: A theoretical concept that doesn't yet exist; often depicted in science fiction

Artificial superintelligence (ASI)

This is AI that surpasses human intelligence, not just in specific tasks, but in virtually every field, including creativity, general wisdom, problem-solving, and social intelligence.

Characteristics:

- *Superiority*: Surpasses the best human brains in virtually every field

- *Autonomous decision-making*: Can make decisions and set its own objectives

- *Self-improvement*: Has the potential for recursive self-improvement, where it can improve its algorithms and structures autonomously

- *Examples*: Theoretical and doesn't exist yet; often the subject of speculative fiction and philosophical discussions, as its realization could lead to profound societal changes

When we are talking about AGI or ASI, there are few things we need to consider.

- *Progression*: It's essential to note that the progression from weak AI to AGI and then ASI isn't just about scaling up. Similar to how NLP moved from RNNs to transformers, this involves foundational advancements in AI algorithms, understanding, and architecture.

- *Timeframe*: Predictions about when (or if) we might achieve AGI or ASI vary widely among experts. Some believe it's just a few decades away, while others think it might take much longer or may never occur at all.

- *Ethical and safety concerns*: As we move toward more advanced forms of AI, ethical and safety concerns intensify. Ensuring that advanced AI aligns with human values can be controlled and is used ethically becomes paramount.

Understanding these levels is important as discussions about AI's societal impact, ethical considerations, and potential become more prevalent. Each level presents its challenges, benefits, and implications.

The emergence of an ASI could bring some unprecedented benefits.

- *Solving complex problems*: Issues like climate change, disease, or even theoretical physics problems could be tackled efficiently.

- *Technological advancements*: Rapid innovation could occur in fields such as space exploration, medicine, energy, and more.

- *Enhanced human abilities*: Through brain-computer interfaces, humans might merge with AI to some extent, enhancing our cognitive abilities.

However, alongside these potential benefits, there are some concerns about existential risks.

Existential Risk from an ASI

An existential risk is one that threatens the extinction of intelligent life or the permanent and drastic reduction of its potential.

These are some of the main existential concerns related to ASI:

- *Loss of control*: Once an ASI system surpasses human intelligence across the board, controlling or predicting its actions becomes challenging. If it's capable of recursive self-improvement, it might quickly evolve in ways we can't foresee or comprehend.

- *Misalignment of values*: Ensuring that an ASI's goals align with human values is a significant challenge. A small misalignment might lead the ASI to take actions that are technically in line with its programmed goals but detrimental to humans.

- *Resource competition*: ASI might see resources that humans rely on as useful for its own goals, leading to competition and potential conflict.

- *Weaponization*: ASI could be used in warfare or by malicious actors, leading to unparalleled destructive capabilities.

- *Dependency and de-skilling*: Over-reliance on ASI could lead to humanity losing essential skills or becoming overly dependent on the technology.

- *Ethical and moral concerns*: Decisions made by ASI, especially those affecting human lives, might not align with our moral and ethical frameworks.

- *Economic disruption*: ASI could render many jobs obsolete, leading to economic and social upheavals.

- *Existential unease*: The mere existence of an entity that surpasses human capabilities in every domain might lead to existential unease or a reevaluation of human purpose and identity.

Apart from these concerns, there are the ethical considerations of the AI itself: if an AI achieves a superintelligent state, questions about its rights and the ethical considerations of its treatment arise. Should it be granted personhood? Would "turning it off" be considered an ethical violation?

Addressing this problem before achieving ASI is crucial because, post-development, we might not get a second chance to make corrections. This requires rigorous research in AI alignment, safety protocols, and ethical guidelines. Some AI researchers advocate for an international collaboration to ensure that the race to develop ASI prioritizes safety over speed. The aim is to ensure that if and when ASI is realized, it benefits all of humanity and doesn't harm or jeopardize our existence.

Where LLMs Fit

Because of the demonstrated abilities of current LLMs, many are assuming them to be ASIs and in turn concerned of the associated existential threats we discussed earlier.

However, this concern is misplaced as LLMs in their current form are not at the capability of ASIs. While they represent a significant advancement in machine learning and natural language processing, they are not examples of artificial superintelligence.

In fact, current LLMs are not even at the AGI level.

For an AI model to reach the AGI level, it needs to be able to understand, learn, and perform any intellectual task that a human can. This means that an AI needs to be able to at least match human cognitive abilities in every area to be considered an AGI. To be considered an ASI, it needs to excel in abilities in every cognitive area.

Current LLMs are good language models and great for text generation and comprehension. But they do not have capabilities beyond that.

However, they can be viewed as steppingstones on the path toward more advanced AI capabilities.

Here are some of the ways LLMs are helping the AI field as a whole to move forward:

- *Demonstration of scalability*: LLMs show that as we increase model size, data, and compute resources, performance on a variety of tasks tends to improve. This suggests that, to some extent, scaling up current techniques might be a viable path to more capable AI systems, though it's uncertain if it will lead directly to ASI.

- *Transfer learning and generalization*: LLMs are trained on diverse datasets and can perform a range of tasks without task-specific training, showcasing the potential of transfer learning. The ability to generalize across tasks is a crucial aspect of AGI and, by extension, ASI.

- *Foundational for more complex systems*: While LLMs are primarily designed for text generation and comprehension, components based on similar architectures could be integrated into more complex AI systems that have multimodal capabilities (handling text, image, video, etc.) or more advanced reasoning abilities.

- *Ethical and safety precedents*: LLMs provide a testing ground for ethical and safety concerns related to AI. Issues like bias in AI outputs, the potential for misuse, and the challenges in specifying desired behavior are all apparent even at the LLM level. Addressing these challenges now helps in preparing for more advanced AI systems.

- *Human-AI interaction*: LLMs offer insights into human-AI collaboration. By using LLMs, we can learn more about how humans and advanced AI systems might coexist, collaborate, and communicate in the future.

It's crucial to differentiate between the capabilities of current LLMs and the theoretical capabilities of ASI. LLMs, no matter how large, don't possess consciousness, self-awareness, or general intelligence that surpasses human capabilities across all fields. They operate based on patterns in the data they were trained on and lack true understanding or reasoning.

The limitations and failures of LLMs can inform AI researchers about the gaps between current technologies and the desired features of AGI or ASI. For instance, LLMs' occasional nonsensical outputs, susceptibility to adversarial inputs, or inability to reason deeply about complex topics highlight areas that need significant advancements.

In summary, while LLMs are not close to ASI, they play a role in the AI research landscape, offering insights, raising important questions, and pushing the boundaries of what machine learning models can achieve. They can be viewed as a piece of the puzzle, helping the AI community understand certain aspects of the journey toward more advanced AI forms.

Misconceptions and Misuse

While we may not need to be concerned about AI taking over the world yet, there are some misconceptions regarding LLMs that may cause either intentional or unintentional misuse.

The following are some of the widely held misconceptions and misunderstandings about LLMs.

LLMs understand content.

- *Misconception*: LLMs understand the text they generate in the same way humans do.

- *Reality*: LLMs don't "understand" content. They generate text based on patterns in the training data but lack a deep or conscious understanding of the concepts they discuss.

139

LLMs are conscious or self-aware.

- *Misconception*: Due to their advanced capabilities, LLMs possess consciousness or self-awareness.

- *Reality*: LLMs are not conscious entities. They process information and generate outputs without awareness, emotions, or intent.

LLMs always produce correct information.

- *Misconception*: Outputs from LLMs are always accurate and trustworthy.

- *Reality*: LLMs can produce incorrect, misleading, or biased information, depending on the prompt and the patterns in their training data.

LLMs are knowledge models.

- *Misconception*: LLMs have knowledge on a vast number of fields; therefore, we can use them as knowledge models.

- *Reality*: LLMs are only as good as their training data, and only able to learn linguistic relationships from them

Bigger is always better.

- *Misconception*: Increasing the size of a model will always lead to better and more accurate results.

- *Reality*: While larger models often exhibit better generalization, there are diminishing returns, and other challenges such as increased computational costs and potential overfitting can arise.

LLMs can invent novel, advanced knowledge.

- *Misconception*: LLMs can create or discover new knowledge, theories, or facts.

- *Reality*: LLMs generate text based on their training data. They can't invent genuinely novel scientific theories or facts beyond the scope of their training.

LLMs are free from bias.

- *Misconception*: LLMs provide objective and unbiased information.

- *Reality*: Since LLMs are trained on vast amounts of Internet text, they can and do inherit biases present in that data.

LLMs can replace all human jobs.

- *Misconception*: Because of their text generation capabilities, LLMs will replace all jobs related to writing, customer service, etc.

- *Reality*: While LLMs can automate some tasks, many jobs require human judgment, creativity, empathy, and context-awareness that LLMs currently lack.

LLMs responses are deliberate or endorsed by their creators.

- *Misconception*: If an LLM generates a particular statement, it reflects the beliefs or intentions of its creators or trainers.

- *Reality*: LLMs generate outputs based on training data patterns, without intent. An output doesn't imply endorsement by the model's creators.

All LLMs are alike.

- *Misconception*: All large language models, irrespective of their architecture or training data, behave similarly.

- *Reality*: Different models, training processes, and fine-tuning can result in varied behavior and capabilities.

Understanding these misconceptions is crucial, especially as LLMs become more integrated into products, services, and decision-making processes. Proper education and communication about what LLMs can and cannot do are essential to harness their potential responsibly.

Researchers have also found that LLMs can suffer from a situation called *hallucinations*. These refer to instances where the model generates information that isn't accurate, grounded in reality, or present in its training data. Essentially, the model "makes things up" or provides outputs that might seem plausible but aren't factual or real.

There can be many reasons for hallucinations.

- *Generalization from training data*: LLMs generalize from their vast training data to answer queries or generate text. While this generalization is often useful, it can sometimes lead the model to create outputs that are not strictly accurate.

- *Lack of ground truth*: Unlike some other AI models that have a clear "ground truth" or correct answer (e.g., an image classifier labeling a picture of a cat), LLMs work in domains where the truth can be more nebulous. This makes it challenging to always generate the "correct" response, especially when the prompt is ambiguous.

- *Bias and incorrect information in training data*: If the model's training data contains misinformation, biases, or outdated information, the model might reproduce or even amplify these inaccuracies in its outputs.

- *Overfitting or memorization*: While LLMs like GPT-3 are designed to generalize rather than memorize, there's always a risk that a model might "remember" and reproduce specific patterns, phrases, or pieces of information from its training data, even if they aren't accurate or relevant to the prompt.

- *User prompt influence*: The way a user crafts a prompt can significantly influence the model's output. Ambiguous or leading prompts can increase the likelihood of hallucinated responses.

- *No external fact-checking mechanism*: LLMs generate responses based on patterns in their training data and don't have the capability to fact-check against external or up-to-date sources in real time.

To address hallucinations, researchers and developers use techniques like fine-tuning on more specific datasets, adding human-in-the-loop review processes, or building external verification systems to cross-check outputs.

Users should always approach outputs from LLMs with a critical mindset, especially when using them for tasks that require high accuracy or have significant real-world implications.

LLMs provide a vast range of positive applications because of their text generation capabilities, but their power also opens the door to potential intentional misuse as well. The following are some of the areas that misuse can happen:

- *Disinformation and fake news*: LLMs can generate believable but entirely fictitious news articles or stories. These can be used to spread false information, manipulate public opinion, or create political instability.

- *Impersonation*: With enough data about a person's writing style, an LLM could be used to generate messages or emails that mimic that individual, leading to potential fraud or misinformation.

- *Automated spam and phishing*: LLMs can craft highly personalized and convincing spam emails, increasing the likelihood of people falling for phishing schemes.

- *Toxic and harmful content*: If not properly controlled, LLMs can produce or amplify harmful, biased, or offensive content.

- *Cheating in education contexts*: Students could use LLMs to automatically generate essays, project reports, or answers to questions, undermining educational integrity.

- *Unfair competition in content creation*: LLMs can be used to mass-produce articles, blog posts, or other written content, potentially flooding platforms with low-cost, generic content and squeezing out human creators.

- *Deepfakes*: While deepfakes primarily involve manipulating videos, the scripts or dialogues for these videos could be generated by LLMs to make them sound more convincing.

- *Stock market manipulation*: By generating fake news or rumors about companies, LLMs could be used to manipulate stock prices for financial gain.

- *Unwanted data extraction*: Users could craftily question LLMs to retrieve specific information from their training data, potentially leading to privacy concerns.

- *Manipulation in social engineering attacks*: Attackers could use LLMs to craft persuasive messages or narratives that trick individuals into revealing personal information or taking actions against their best interests.

- *Intensifying echo chambers*: By providing content that aligns with users' existing beliefs (based on input data), LLMs could further entrench individuals in their echo chambers, exacerbating polarization.

Recognizing these potential misuses is the first step in creating safeguards. Developers and platforms using LLMs should be aware of these risks and employ measures to prevent them, such as fine-tuning models for safety, adding layers of human review, or setting guidelines for responsible usage.

Opportunities

Large language models have introduced a myriad of opportunities across various domains because of their advanced text generation capabilities. Here are some handful of examples from a wide array of possibilities.

Content creation assistance

- LLMs can help writers generate ideas, structure content, or even write drafts. And they can assist in poetry, storytelling, scriptwriting, and other forms of creative expression to supplement human created content rather than to replace them.

Education

- *Tutoring*: LLMs can offer personalized explanations on a range of topics, helping students understand complex concepts.

- *Language learning*: They can assist language learners by offering translations, explanations, or conversational practice.

Research and information gathering

- LLMs can summarize large amounts of text, generate literature reviews, or help researchers explore various perspectives on a topic.

Business applications

- *Customer support*: The can automate responses to frequently asked questions or guiding users through troubleshooting.

- *Drafting emails*: The can assist professionals in crafting well-structured and articulated emails or reports.

Programming and development

- *Code generation*: Given a human-readable prompt, LLMs can generate code snippets or even assist in debugging.

Gaming

- LLMs can be used to generate dialogue for characters, create dynamic storylines, or even craft entire in-game worlds based on textual descriptions.

Entertainment

- They can create dialogue for movies, generate plot ideas, or assist in scriptwriting.

Human-computer interaction

- With LLMs, the interaction between users and software can become more natural, with the software better understanding and generating human-like text.

Accessibility

- LLMs can be used to develop advanced chatbots for individuals who may need companionship or support, or they can translate complex text into simpler language for individuals with different cognitive needs.

Cultural preservation

- LLMs trained on diverse datasets can help in preserving and sharing knowledge about various cultures, languages, and traditions that might be less represented online.

Idea generation and brainstorming

- They can assist teams in coming up with creative solutions, product names, or marketing strategies.

Mental health and well-being

- While not a replacement for professional therapy, LLMs can be used as interactive journaling tools, offering responses or reflections based on user input.

While these opportunities are exciting, it's crucial to use LLMs responsibly. Ensuring the generated content aligns with human values is factually accurate (where necessary) and doesn't unintentionally propagate biases or misinformation is essential. Moreover, in areas such as mental health, LLMs should be used with caution, always underlining the importance of human expertise and intervention.

Summary

As with the introduction of any new technology, LLMs have given rise to a set of concerns and perceived threats. Most of these concerns are due to not understanding what LLMs truly are. However, there are genuine concerns as well. The capabilities of LLMs can be misused—either intentionally or not—that may have negative impacts in our day-to-day lives. As LLMs technologies become more common, it is important to understand these risks and add safeguards to prevent them.

As we are still at the beginning of the LLM era, we may see new opportunities, approaches, and entire industries emerge around them in the near future.

Large language models are a milestone in artificial intelligence and human ingenuity. It is our responsibility to use them correctly and rationally to ensure progress and a bright future for all.

Index

A

Accessibility, 147
Add-one smoothing, 41, 42
Adversarial training, 104
Artificial general intelligence (AGI), 133, 137
Artificial intelligence (AI), 3
  AGI, 133
  ASI, 134
  democratization, 109
  generative AI, 6
  landscape, 7
  LLMs, 138, 139
  ML, 4
  model training, 5
  narrow/weak AI, 133
  optimism, 3
  repositories, 130
  subfields, 3
Artificial neural networks (ANNs), 4
Artificial superintelligence (ASI)
  benefits, 135
  characteristics, 134
  considerations, 134, 135

existential risk, 135–137
Attention mechanism, 56, 64
  key vectors, 58
  query vector, 58
  scores, 59, 60
  softmax function, 59
  value vectors, 59
  weighted sum, 59
Audio-text association, 103
Autoencoding models, 91
  applications, 96
  bidirectional context, 95
  limitations, 96, 97
  masked language modeling, 95
  parallelism, 95
  training, 95
Autoregression, 91
Autoregressive models, 91
  applications, 93, 94
  causal relationship, 92
  context understanding, 92
  limitations, 94
  long-range dependencies, 92
  sequence generation, 92
  training process, 93

© Thimira Amaratunga 2023
T. Amaratunga, *Understanding Large Language Models*,
https://doi.org/10.1007/979-8-8688-0017-7

Printed in the United States
by Baker & Taylor Publisher Services